RETIREMENT MATTERS FOR MINISTERS

A report on a research project into how
Baptist ministers experience retirement

RETIREMENT MATTERS FOR MINISTERS

A report on a research project into how
Baptist ministers experience retirement

Paul Beasley-Murray

Published in 2018 by The College of Baptist Ministers

CBM
college of baptist ministers

RETIREMENT MATTERS FOR MINISTERS

A report on a research project into how Baptist ministers experience retirement

ISBN NUMBER 978-1-9165035-0-2

First published in 2018 by The College of Baptist Ministers

Company Limited by Guarantee number 8419543 registered in England and Wales at 1 Mimosa Close Chelmsford CM1 6NW.

This booklet is dedicated to my fellow retired Baptist ministers. I wish too to express my appreciation to all those who filled in the questionnaires – and in particular to the seventeen ministers who allowed me to conduct lengthy interviews with them.

CONTENTS

INTRODUCTION

A dearth of writing on how ministers experience retirement

Although there are many books written on ministerial retirement from a North American perspective,[1] there is little from a distinctively British perspective. The only book I have come across in the UK is *Pastors under Pressure: Conflicts on the outside, fears within* by James Taylor, a Scottish Baptist minister, who devoted a third of a more general book on ministry to retirement issues. [2]

The journal of the Baptist Ministers' Fellowship – formerly the *Fraternal* and now the *Baptist Ministers Journal* - has in forty years published seven articles on various aspects of retirement.[3] Over a twenty-four year period the journal *Ministry Today* similarly published several thought-provoking contributions on

---

[1] For instance: Paul C. Clayton, *Called for Life: Finding Meaning in Retirement* (Alban Institute, Herndon, Virginia 2008); Gwen Wagstrom Halaas, *Clergy, Retirement and Wholeness: Looking Forward to the Third Age* (Alban, Herndon, Virginia 2005); Daniel A. Roberts & Michael Friedman, *Clergy Retirement: Every ending a new beginning for clergy, their families and congregants* (Bayswood Publishing Company, 2016; and then Routledge, London & New York 2017); also Bruce & Katherine Epperly, *Four Seasons of Ministry: Gathering a Harvest of Righteousness* (Alban, Herndon, Virginia 2008).

[2] James Taylor, *Pastors under Pressure: Conflicts on the outside, fears within* (Day One Publications, Leominster, 2nd edition 2001)

[3] Charles Johnson, 'What can a retired minister contribute to the church?, *Fraternal* 167 (May 1973) 3-31; Norman Jones, 'One man's retirement', *Fraternal* 190 (January 1980) 19-23; Derek Rumbol, 'Looking forward to what is to come', *BMJ* 266 (April 1999) 10-13; Anon (Michael Ball?), 'Release from ministry: a pre-retirement liturgy', *BMJ* 280 (October 2002) 11-12; David Baker, 'Adjustments in retirement', *BMJ* 293 (January 2006) 25-27; Philip Clements-Jewery, 'A retirement retreat', *BMJ* 309 (January 2011) 21-22; David Doonan, 'Incarnational retirement ministry', *BMJ 313* (January 2012) 19-22.

retirement. [4] I myself wrote two articles on retirement for *Ministry Today*. [5] In addition, I wrote a major section about retirement in *Living Out the Call: Book One Living to God's Glory*, [6] and devoted some of my *Church Matters* blogs to the theme. [7] More recently I have reflected on my experience of retirement in the penultimate chapter of *This is my story: a story of life, faith and ministry*. [8] However, I am conscious that I was for the most part drawing upon my experience, as distinct from drawing on any 'hard' data.

The purpose of my research

This was the context in which I decided to undertake a survey of retired Baptist ministers. One of my concerns was that there appeared to be little pastoral care for Baptist ministers once they retire. Undoubtedly some retired ministers settle down happily in a church, where they are well cared for by the pastor. However, I had come across instances where that was not the case: retired ministers had told me how marginalised they felt in their local churches; others I discovered had on retirement made their spiritual home in a church of another denomination.

---

[4] Jim Hamilton, 'Do ministers really retire?', *Ministry Today* 57 (Spring 2013) 18-22; Paul Goodliff, 'Approaching retirement', *Ministry Today* 57 (Spring 2013) 23-28; Andrew Knowles, 'Coming in to land', *Ministry Today* 59 (Autumn 2013) 17-22; Keith Clements, 'Seven virtues for retired ministers', *Ministry Today* 63 (Spring 2015) 40-42.

[5] See Paul Beasley-Murray, 'Editorial: Retirement? Not yet!', *Ministry Today* 43 (Summer 2008) 4-5; 'Growing old: some preliminary thoughts', *Ministry Today* 60 (Spring 2014) 36-39.

[6] See *Living Out the Call: 1. Living to God's Glory* (Feed-a-Read, 2nd edition 2016; also available as an e-book) 'Ministry beyond Retirement' 92-99.

[7] Paul Beasley-Murray, *Church Matters*: 'Retirement wishes' (1 May 2014); 'Seven virtues for retired ministers' (15 January 2015); 'There is a time to stand down' (23 April 2015); 'Do we ever retire?' (9 June 2016); 'A new ministry' (30 June 2016); and 'Retiring Retirement' (18 May 2017). See www.paulbeasleymurray.com.

[8] *This is my story: a story of life, faith and ministry* (Wipf & Stock, Eugene, Oregon 2018).

But these were all individual stories – as far as I was aware, there were no statistics upon which to draw.

I was also interested to discover how Baptist ministers experience retirement in general. James Taylor in *Pastors under Pressure* painted a somewhat negative picture of retirement. It is a picture which I did not recognise. My experience of retirement has been very positive. But is my experience of retirement less typical than his? This too was something which I wanted to explore.

I hoped, too, that my research into ministerial retirement might prove a help into enabling Baptist churches and associations to become more effective in the pastoral care they offer to ministers.

Research methodology

My first thought was to send out a questionnaire to all retired Baptist ministers in the Baptist Union of Great Britain. Although a daunting project, I knew from my own experience that technically such a survey would be possible. [9] However, after consulting with friends, I was persuaded that a different approach was needed. Instead of a large-scale 'quantitative' research project, I opted to engage in some 'qualitative' research and conduct a series of face-to-face interviews, supported by some limited 'quantitative' research.

---

[9] Over the years I have engaged in three major surveys. While in my first church in Altrincham I wrote to every other Baptist church with a membership of 50 or more with a view to testing out Peter Wagner's theories relating to church growth: the results of the 350 churches who responded were analysed and published in *Turning the Tide: an assessment of Baptist church growth in England* (Bible Society, London 1981). In my second church in Chelmsford I conducted a survey relating to the use and abuse of power in the local church: 141 ministers and 112 church officers from the mainline Protestant churches responded and the results of that survey were published in *Power for God's Sake* (Paternoster, Carlisle 1998). In my retirement, with the help of regional team leaders, I sent out a questionnaire to almost 2000 ministers about their reading habits: over 300 ministers responded and the results were published in the *Baptist Quarterly* 49.1 (January 2018).

After testing a prototype, I produced a lengthy questionnaire (16 sides of A4) which included a good number of open-ended questions. My aim in the first place was to use this questionnaire as the basis of face-to-face interviews with ministers living in the Eastern Baptist Association, which covers the area in which my home city of Chelmsford is found. I ended up having seventeen in-depth interviews, most of which were two to three hours in length, with Baptist ministers living in Essex, Norfolk, and Suffolk. Some may be a little surprised to discover that the seventeen included no women: this simply reflects the fact that in the Eastern Baptist Association almost all retired ministers are men.

At the same time, I sent out questionnaires to a larger random group of retired Baptist ministers who live at a distance from Chelmsford. This larger group consisted of nine more retired ministers from the Eastern Baptist Association, and a further twenty-seven retired ministers from most of the other associations within the Baptist Union.[10] Of the twenty-seven ministers outside the Eastern Baptist Association, three were women. In total, including the seventeen questionnaires completed by the retired ministers who I interviewed, I received fifty-three questionnaires to analyse.

As at 4 December 2017, there were 896 retired Baptist ministers in the Baptist pension scheme. If we add those Baptist ministers not in the scheme, then there must be somewhere between 900-1000 retired Baptist ministers. In other words, around a third of Baptist ministers in the Baptist Union of Great Britain are retired! The 53 respondents therefore represent just over 5% of all retired Baptist ministers. To what extent the experience of this sample is representative

---

[10] These 27 came from the following Baptist associations: Central (1); East Midlands (8); Heart of England (3); London (1); South Eastern (3); South Wales (2); South West (2); Southern Counties (2); West of England (1); Yorkshire (2). No questionnaires were received from the North Western and the Northern associations.

of retired Baptist ministers is a matter for the statisticians to debate! [11]

The division of the book

The first main section, Encounters with Ministry 'Heroes', contains a summary of the seventeen interviews I had with retired ministers. In order to keep the identities of the ministers confidential I have used pseudonyms; I have also been deliberately vague in giving details relating to their past ministries and their present circumstances. In most cases the wives were present for the interviews.

The second main section, 'The Retirement Experience' is devoted to analysing the data from the questionnaires. In terms of presentation, I have followed advice and adopted the general practice of putting the 'raw data' in a series of tables in an appendix. For the sake of objectivity, I have sought to ensure that my comments do not reflect my own views.

The third main section, 'Retired Ministers Matter', deals with results relating to one key aspect of the research. There are other issues which are also important, some of which could well have implications for the Baptist Union retirement course.

---

[11] The survey results reflect the whole population with a margin of error of plus or minus 13% (to a confidence level of 95%). Recognising this, results have only been reported if they are statistically significant.

SECTION ONE: ENCOUNTERS WITH MINISTRY 'HEROES': A REPORT ON 17 INTERVIEWS

At the heart of the research project were visits to seventeen retired Baptist ministers resident in Essex, Suffolk and Norfolk – all within the area covered by the Eastern Baptist Association. I use the term 'visits' advisedly. Elsewhere I speak of 'face-to-face' interviews. However, what really counted was that with three exceptions the interviews took place within people's own homes. After a life-time of visiting others, they were now receiving a pastoral visit.

In the past as a minister of a local church I rarely spent more than forty minutes for a pastoral visit. However, on these occasions I set aside two to three hours for each visit. This was deliberate. I needed time to connect – or in some cases reconnect – with each minister, which I did by asking them to tell me about their experience of ministry. I also needed time to talk through their responses to my questionnaire, with a view to discovering the issues which really concerned them. In addition, I wanted to express my personal thanks to each minister for their ministry. To each minister I said:

"Even if the whole exercise proves worthless, the visiting of ministers in their homes will have had value. Although most ministers will have concluded their ministry with a service of celebration, I do not believe that their contribution to the life of our churches has been sufficiently valued. Most ministers have loved their people and have given of themselves unstintingly to their people – sadly most past ministers are soon forgotten – and as this survey goes on to show, a good number of retired ministers feel forgotten ('unrecognised'; 'abandoned'). In my own right and as chairman of the College of Baptist Ministers I want to say a massive thank you."

In reporting on my visits, I do not intend to reproduce all the information contained in their responses – that is contained in the subsequent analysis of the questionnaires. Instead I want to highlight the issues which they thought important. In that regard it was important for me not to steer the conversations in any one direction – but rather to allow the ministers themselves to speak. Without exception the conversations were wide-ranging. Yet, as will be seen, often there was a commonality of theme.

It was a real privilege visiting these seventeen retired ministers as also their wives (apart from the two who had been widowed). Without exception they were open and honest with me as they talked about themselves. But it was more than a privilege – it was also an amazing experience. For to my surprise I discovered that each one of them, in their own different way, was a 'hero' of the faith. Perhaps because at the time I was preparing a series of Bible studies on the Letter to the Hebrews, I was vividly reminded of Hebrews 11 with its roll call of past heroes of the faith, and realised that in my visits I was encountering some of today's heroes of the faith!

Drawing upon the literary style of Hebrews 11 I wrote: "By faith they set out in ministry not knowing where the journey would lead them – by faith they lived in homes not their own – by faith they offered up their wives and children in the service of God – by faith they climbed the mountains , but also plumbed the depths of human experience – by faith they preached the good news and lived out the life of the kingdom – by faith they saw their churches grow, but they also saw their churches decline – by faith they experienced the love of their people, and by faith they experienced rejection and misunderstanding......".

Listening to their stories, I was overwhelmed by a sense of respect and admiration for these ministers who had known some of the highs, but also some of the lows in Christian ministry. I remember the day, when in the morning one minister had told me of how he had been effectively forced to resign from one church – and then in the afternoon listening to another minister tell me how he had been sacked from one church and then had to resign from another church. Neither of these men were in my judgment problem ministers – rather they had encountered problem churches – and all too often problem leaders.[12] In the course of such ministries, many had been wounded – but in the words of the title of book written many years ago by Marjory Foyle, they had been 'honourably wounded'. [13] Sadly today these 'heroes' are unknown to most today – but thankfully they are 'known to God'.

One further point needs to be made: it will be seen that none of the seventeen ministers with whom I met were women. This reflects the fact that in the Eastern Baptist Association retired women Baptist ministers are a rarity: – as far as I am aware there is just one elderly woman minister who began as a 'deaconess' in 1952, who retired as long ago as 1987 and is now not in the best of health.

Anthony

Anthony came into ministry having worked in theatre stage design and taught art in a public school. He retired at 65 after over twenty-one years as a Baptist minister. He had two ministries – and four churches.

In his first ministry his task was to bring two churches together. There was a good deal of antagonism between the churches – one in particular had a reputation in the town for being 'the church that says no'. It was hard work, but in the end the two churches came together.

In his second ministry, he had a similar task of bringing together two churches that "could not stand the sight of one another". He felt a real sense of achievement when these two churches became "one new church". Unfortunately, the new church went against his advice and instead of opting to be a 'neighbourhood' church surrounded by homes, they refurbished an old building in the centre of town. In Anthony's opinion they

---

[12] In *Power for God's Sake: the use and abuse of power in the local church* (Paternoster, Carlisle 1998) 102 I reported that 53% of Baptist ministers said that their predecessor had left 'in unhappy circumstances'.

[13] Marjorie Foyle, *Honourably Wounded: Stress among Christian workers* (Marc Europe 1987). It was primarily written with missionaries in mind – but it could equally be written of Christian ministers!

sold the wrong set of premises and effectively turned their back on a great mission opportunity.

In spite of good things, both his ministries proved to be highly demanding – and were characterised by much antagonism within each church. Anthony found his second ministry the most difficult – the situation was made more complicated by his predecessor returning to the church almost every Friday. Not surprisingly he stated in the questionnaire, "There were good times, but there were difficult times too".

Although he and his wife were a warm and outgoing couple, in none of his churches were they able to make real friends – instead they had the pain of seeing friendships they thought they had made being betrayed. Indeed, as Anthony looks back on his ministerial formation and career, he can only think of one person whom he can unreservedly trust.

Retirement was traumatic for Anthony – not only did retirement mean he lost his role, his home, and many of his possessions (for like most retired ministers he had to radically down-size when he left the church manse) he also lost his wife in the week running up to his retirement. The planned service of thanksgiving for his ministry was cancelled, and instead there was his wife's funeral. He still finds it hard to come to terms with never having experienced retirement with his wife. As he said to me, "You don't get over a loss, you learn only how to cope with it".

On retirement Anthony moved to be near his daughter, who was diagnosed with MS just before his wife died. However, when his daughter moved many miles away with her partner, he decided to move again to be near the support group of the hospice which had cared for his wife. He has ended up as an informal chaplain to the thirty or so people in this support group.

Both his children have had problems with their marriages, with the result that Anthony feels that he is having to care for them rather than they care for him.

Financially things are tough. For Anthony's wife, instead of pursuing a career while he was in ministry, threw herself into church work. Anthony's pension is therefore under £20,000. He says that he is "just about managing". He has a very small house from the Retired Baptist Minsters Housing Society (RBMHS), which means that one tenth of his total pension goes on 'rent'.

Anthony has got involved in a local church – and has done a fair amount of preaching for the church. He is "very happy" in the church, and feels the church is "very supportive" to him. He has also a host of wider interests – he belongs to a walking group and to a choir, he has gone to ballroom dancing lessons, he paints, and he often goes to the theatre or the cinema. However, after five years of retirement, he is struggling with the question of "Who am I now?". He felt he could not answer any of the questions relating to general reflections on his experience of retirement. He is still searching for purpose.

Anthony is a man in need of some specialist support – but there is none. After a lifetime of active engagement with the Baptist denomination, he feels "forgotten by the wider Baptist family" – indeed, he says that he has been "abandoned". He has not had a pastoral visit or a personal letter or a phone call from his regional minister – and does not even know the name of the local regional minister. He is, however, grateful for the support he receives from the retired ministers group to which he belongs

In addition, he is concerned that Baptists are not taking advantage of the vast experience represented by retired ministers: "we have a vast library of gathered ministerial knowledge that is left untapped for the most part". It is important to say that Anthony is not a natural 'grumbler' – as I know from my previous knowledge of him he is a positive, interesting character, who is not slow to express appreciation. However, he feels deeply wounded by the lack of support from the Baptist Union and the Association.

Ben

Ben is a practical guy and trained as an electronics engineer. In response to God's call he started his training for ministry at the age of 23. Very much a 'pastor-teacher' he pastored five churches.

Ben's first church was stuck in the past and found change difficult. When he began there were some fifty-five members, but under his leadership the church grew. Sadly the next minister 'blew the church apart', and many of those who helped left for other churches. At that stage, he said, I learnt that 'the kingdom' is bigger than one local church.

His second church was a very happy church which responded well to his ministry. When Ben was diagnosed with leukaemia, the church really cared for him.

Ben then moved to a growing market town, where the church underwent a period of massive growth. This was "the peak" of his ministry. The youth work was "stunning", with 80-100 young people at the Sunday services. But for all the excitement, there was a darker side. A small group of "awkward customers" gave Ben and his wife "hell": in their pursuit of power and control they undermined his leadership and in the process almost destroyed the church.

Ben moved on again, this time to a much smaller church whose premises had been burnt down some years previously. Redevelopment plans had stalled, but with his encouragement they built a 'community-style' building. It was at this time that Ben's wife's health began to seriously deteriorate, and Ben found himself having to cope with the tension of both pastoring a church and also caring for a sick wife.

Realising he needed a less demanding church, he moved yet again and found himself on a rough London overspill estate, where the members were locked in the past and refused to change. His wife got worse and suffered a series of life-threatening incidents: for all that time she was wheel-chair bound and at one stage had to spend eight months in hospital. Eventually Ben realised could not remain in 'active' ministry, and so at the age of 63 he retired. Although his wife still has major health issues, thankfully she is now on longer wheel-chair bound, but nonetheless Ben is still her carer

Ben and his wife are now living happily and fruitfully in retirement. They chose to live in a small town with a lively church, and with this choice in mind the RBMHS was able to provide a delightful bungalow – the bungalow cost £17,000 more than the RBMHS purchase limit, but Ben's father was able to plug the gap with the gift of an early 'legacy'. Ben is very grateful to God for the work of the RBMHS.

Their combined income is around £25,000 and so they have to be careful with their money. Nonetheless, by shopping around say they are "content and comfortable".

They have made many good friends in their new church – and have consciously made an effort to develop friends outside the church. For Ben working on the development and now the maintenance of new church premises has been a good means of bonding.

Adjusting to retirement has taken several years for Ben. One of the challenges he faces is finding the right balance between making time for others and time for himself and his wife. In this regard they ensure that Monday is their 'day off', when they have quality time with one another. He says that in retirement he is still "searching for purpose", in the sense that he continues to discover the kind of person that God would have him be.

They are grateful for the "more than adequate" pastoral care of the church and for the regular contact they have with other retired ministers through a group for retired ministers. Ben is not content with the lack of pastoral support from the Baptist Union and the association – and, as with many others, has never had a pastoral visit or personal letter or phone call from a regional minister. Nonetheless he still feels he is "part of the wider Baptist family".

Bruce

Bruce began his working life in a family bakery, before becoming the main buyer for a hardware warehouse. After training for the ministry, his first church was in a navy town at the time of the Falklands conflict: he describes it as a busy but difficult period. He moved on to hospital chaplaincy, where he enjoyed engaging with 'normal' people – as distinct from church people. This was followed by a spell pastoring two small churches, ten miles apart, but after eight years the money ran out and he had to look for another church. In his next church he initially went "through hell" when he had to stand up to the bullying tactics of one deacon – but after her resignation things improved and he led the church through a programme of major renovation. His last church was a large black church, where he and his wife were the only white members – he enjoyed the challenge of pastoring what was in many ways the equivalent of a Jamaican 'parish' church.

Yet although there were high points in every church, in every church there were also low points, all of which centred around what Bruce called 'internal church politics'. His motives were frequently challenged as he sought to bring about change – "are you doing this for the good of the church, pastor?" Time and again people sought to promote their own agenda as he tried to take the church forward. Bruce loved preaching and pastoring – but not church meetings! For him ministry "was tough and often unrewarding".

After thirty-eight years in stipendiary ministry retirement came as a massive 'relief' – unlike so many of his former peers who had become casualties in ministry, he had made it safely to the end. Other emotions included 'depression' caused partly by serious ill-health in the last year of his ministry – in that respect he did not finish as well as he had hoped. He also experienced considerable 'frustration' because he and his wife had to stay on an extra seven months in the manse, as they waited for a RBMHS house to become available.

Retirement has proved a disappointment. To his surprise he has more time on his hands than he wants – indeed, he would say that he is "still looking for a purpose" in retirement. He describes 'boredom' as the hardest challenge he has faced in retirement. After almost three years he has yet to "settle". He preaches around, but that does not seem to bring him much satisfaction. He does, however, enjoy helping with a local wild-life trust, where his voluntary work involves clearing brambles and putting up fences to look after the sheep.

His local Baptist church has proved less than welcoming. His wife has had major health issues, but there has been little understanding on the part of the church. He tells the story of bringing his wife to a Sunday service in a wheel chair: he moved one chair to make room for his wife's wheel chair only to be told that it was "Mrs so-and-so's seat". He therefore went to move another chair, only to be told that it was somebody else's seat. At that point he decided there was no point staying on for the service!

The last three years have been really tough relating to the church. Over the past six months they have not been invited out by any church members – this is strange because I found Bruce and his wife the most warm of couples. The few 'friends' they have made in the church have been little more than acquaintances. He feels very much on the edge of the church. Retirement, he says, "has proved a lonely experience".

Fortunately he and his wife are beginning to build relationships with their non-church neighbours. They are also great friends ("we can drop in on one another without notice") with an old ministerial 'buddy' and his wife, and in some ways this retired minister serves as a mentor to Bruce.

Although a member of the local Baptist church, Bruce has begun to worship more often at a nearby Anglican church, where he finds greater depth and more stimulation.

Bruce could do with some real support. He has received no support from any regional minister – no visit, no letter, and no phone call. Much as he appreciates living in a RBMHS house, he is surprised he has received no pastoral support from that organisation either. After a life-time of service in Baptist churches, he feels discarded. Still a convinced Baptist, when it comes to the wider 'Baptist family, he now feels "neither one thing nor another".

Edward

Edward is a competent, intelligent and reflective minister. In response to the call of God he turned his back on a promising chemistry career, and trained for the ministry, in the course of which he spent a year in the USA.

Over thirty-five years he served in four churches during which was always a "gear changer", enabling churches to move on in their mission and ministry.

His first church was a middle of the road traditional church. Under his leadership youth work was started and a mid-week programme was developed. There were conversions and there was growth: it was a happy church, and a great place to "cut one's teeth".

His second church too proved to be a good experience. Although Edward is no 'wild charismatic', the church began to "move in renewal". People young and old came to faith, and the church really grew. Not all was sweetness and light – some high-powered commuters were at times were unreasonable in their expectations. But overall, things went well.

In his third church he experienced conflict and opposition from a group of leaders who wanted things 'their way'. It was Edward's first experience of people going behind his back to undermine his ministry and feed others with "distorted and subversive" information. These leaders called a vote of confidence in Edward – although he won the vote immense damage was done. Mediators were brought in at great expense, but for little gain. Although Edward felt he left well, his wife found it most difficult – she would have gladly walked out of the church, had she been able to!

Edward's last ministry was in a village church with several hundred members. When he arrived, the church had gone through a major church split. Edward was able to lead the church forward and helped it to recover. It was for him too a "really good time".

Over the past eight years Edward and his wife have found it difficult adjusting to retirement. They had difficulties with the house they bought, they were not initially enamoured with their new church (it took them over six years to become members), and Edward's wife in particular missed her old friends enormously. However, they now have quite a number of friends in the church, and in the last six months have been invited into some five homes for a meal. Edward has a "very good" relationship with the minister and feels the church is now supportive.

Edward has not had any pastoral visit or personal letter or phone call from his regional minister; and as far as his relationship with the wider Baptist family is concerned, he feels "neither one thing nor another".

Overall, he says that "retirement has given me new opportunities to serve God", both in his local church, as also through mentoring a few younger ministers.

Their combined annual income is under £20k, but Edward says "I am comfortable"

Frank

Frank began his working life in shipping – and at one stage was responsible for booking passages to Australia for the '£10 Poms'. He went to college at the age of twenty-five and ended up spending almost forty years in stipendiary ministry.

Frank is in his late 70s and has had a range of churches and appointments. His happiest ministry was his first church, where he was the first full-time minister for forty years. It was a "very loving" church. His next church was also a happy experience – he had the joy of baptising many gifted young people; but he also had to deal with the fallout of two painful divorces, as well as cope with all kinds of theological tensions. After fifteen years he felt he needed a break and moved to lead a Christian adventure centre, but after two years he was back in local ministry, and over the next thirteen years he pastored two further churches. Then he was called by his association to be a superintendent/regional minister. He spent his final three years as the senior minister of a large Baptist church which needed an experienced leader to guide them.

When he retired, Frank wanted to live somewhere near to London, where his children live. Initially all that the RBMHS could offer was a house 100 miles from London; later the RBMHS managed to find a house 55 miles from London.

Retirement for Frank has in some ways been a "disappointment" and he has found it difficult to fit into Baptist life. The first Baptist church he belonged to in retirement was still recovering from a church split and was not the happiest of places; the next Baptist church in the town nearer to London was in turmoil, with the minister wanting to conduct 'gay marriages'. Neither church was interested in what Frank had to offer. Frank's experience is that "Baptist churches do not know how, or even do not want, to welcome retired ministers". Frank and his wife now worship in an evangelical Anglican church, where Frank has a "very good" relationship with the minister. Although not enthusiastic about the church (it's "OK"), it has proved to be supportive and they now "feel quite part of the church". They have made friends in the church – and in the past six months five couples have invited them into their home. In terms of his relationship with the 'wider Baptist family', he now feels "neither one thing nor another".

Church apart, Frank has attended study courses linked with the University of the Third Age; he goes occasionally to the cinema and the concert hall; and enjoys photography and building a model-railway. He has also enjoyed a "little travel".

Frank has a passion for "biblical truth". Together with others he has set up an annual 'Bible convention' in the town in which they live. He sees a great need for teaching – house groups are "inadequate" and offer "little in-depth study".

As he looks back on his experience of retirement, the best thing he enjoys is "no pressure on time, or demands on (reduced) energy levels". The hardest challenge he has had to face is "having something to offer when it is not apparently accepted".

John

John began his working life in WH Smiths, and then spent six years as a tailor – he still cuts a dapper figure. After training for the ministry he pastored six churches, retiring after thirty years of service at the age of 65.

John first pastoral charge was to care for two churches set in an idyllic part of the country: one was a growing church with lots of young families, and the other was a collection of elderly 'faithfuls' which ultimately had to close. He then moved to a more industrial setting, where leading the church proved much more challenging. Life was made all the more difficult by a 'narrow-minded' deacon who was determined to wreck the church's ecumenical partnership.

John's next appointment proved a tough assignment. Called to be an associate minister in a larger Baptist church, the senior minister seemed to have no idea of what team ministry was all about, and often undermined and even bullied his colleague. The weekly team meetings became a nightmare – and without supportive friends in the church, John might not have kept going. Even now, many years later, John can vividly recall some of the details of that time – how upset his wife was, and how angry he too eventually became.

Thankfully his final two churches proved much happier. There still were problem people, but he was blessed with good deacons. As he looked back on his ministry, he said that "for the most part" his experience of ministry "was rewarding, but there were tough times too".

Retirement for John proved initially somewhat traumatic. After having given unstintingly of himself in ministry, in which he had shared his life with his people, he felt a massive loss of identity. It was not so much a loss of status, but rather the loss of a role. Even now, happily settled in a local church, he asks, "Who am I?" In one of his responses he said: "I am still searching for purpose". In many ways he lives a full life: not only is he active in the church, he also often goes up to London to visit a theatre or an art gallery, or to listen to a concert. Keen on photography, he also belongs to a local male-voice choir. However, he struggles to know how God would have him use his time.

In terms of pension he and his wife receive in total less than £20,000. If his wife had kept up her career, they would now be receiving a considerably pension – but instead she became a 'full-time" minister's wife. They say, however, they have "enough to live on". They are particularly grateful to the RBMHS for the bungalow they live in – and for the "security" which it brings to them.

With sadness he admits that he feels "forgotten by the wider Baptist family" and is disappointed he has received no pastoral visit or personal letter or phone call from his regional minister. He would like to see retired ministers included in the Association directory of ministers and churches – and for retired ministers to be given a copy.

Lee

Lee is one of the happiest retired ministers I have met – not least because he received a legacy of £100,000 which together with a small mortgage enabled him to buy a delightful cottage. Before he became a Baptist minister, he had a property – but sold it to finance his training for ministry. From his knowledge of other ministers, he is aware of the financial struggles many retired ministers experience. He would love to see churches enabling their ministers to make provision for their retirement – but sees no easy answers to how this might be achieved.

Lee is also blessed because he has settled very happily into his local Baptist church. He is involved in house groups and 'gets his hands dirty' by helping with the coffee rota. In the last six month eight couples have invited him and his wife into their homes for a meal – the folk in this local church appear to be far more hospitable than were his previous churches.

Lee had ten years in accountancy, before training for the ministry. During almost thirty years of ministry, he had three churches. His first ministry was tough because the church had lots of money in the bank, but little sense of mission. The church was comfortable, and simply wanted Lee to be its chaplain. So after just three years, Lee decided to move to a church which shared his vision for reaching out to the community.

His second church was probably his most enjoyable. As minister of an estate church in a rapidly growing new town, Lee had an effective ministry to young families and young people and experienced substantial growth.

His third church was the most challenging. A large established church it went through major leadership changes, and much church meeting time was devoted to church matters, rather than to 'kingdom' matters. There were some low points, which included "church 'politics' vying for power and position and experiencing bullying"; "taking decisions for the good of the church the reason for which could not be shared with the wider church and being misunderstood". Things were tough – and Lee says that without a real sense of call and the public affirmation of that sense of call in ordination, he might well have come un-stuck. In addition, Lee's early experience of managing an accountancy office proved helpful and difficulties, many of which had their roots in an unhelpful leadership structure developed during the interregnum, were resolved. Lee left his final church in a good place.

Retirement is also a 'good place' for Lee. He and his wife are delighted with their new home, set in a quiet spot in the centre of the town. Although their combined income is less than £30,000, they are living within their means and are "comfortable".

In addition they feel "very much part" of their new church. They received a warm welcome and have already made a number of friends. They have been encouraged to use their gifts, with the result that Lee preaches in the church from time to time and is leading an Alpha course. They attend church meetings and "share generally in the life of the church". Lee has a "very good" relationship with the minister, who is secure in himself and does not find having a retired minister in his church a threat –

Lee commented that difficulties arise when the pastor has a 'frail ego'.

After years of being out almost every night on church business, Lee is keen now to do things together with his wife in the wider community. They have joined the local Arts Society, and Lee is exploring the possibility of becoming a Rotarian.

Since retiring Lee has not had "a pastoral visit or personal letter or phone call" from his regional minister. However, that does not worry Lee. He and his wife feel cared for in their new church. Although previously highly involved in denominational life, Lee feels somewhat disillusioned now. In terms of feeling part of the wider 'Baptist family', Lee says he feels "neither one thing nor another".

For Lee, the best thing about retirement is "not having responsibility and freedom to choose activities and plan the day". The hardest challenge is "relaxing and thinking I'm not wasting time". He is still passionate about "seeing people reach their full potential in Christ".

Leslie

Leslie still has great energy and drive. Before training for the ministry he spent ten years in accountancy, and perhaps as a result has always shown great entrepreneurial flair.

Leslie served for over thirty years in stipendiary ministry – and then after eleven years of retirement (where he became church secretary of his local Baptist church) he went back into pastoral ministry for a further four years, finally retiring only because of his wife's health.

Leslie looks back on a life that has been "exciting, challenging and very rewarding". All his ministries, he says, have been good, but none matched his first church, where he had a "brilliant" all-round ministry: the church grew substantially and became involved with people suffering with mental health problems with Leslie setting up a small housing association with nineteen properties. There were "no low points" in his first church!

Leslie moved on for a brief while into a denominational position – there it was not church members, but some 'area superintendents' (precursors of regional ministers) who gave him problems. On his return to pastoral ministry, Leslie went to a struggling city centre church for a few years – although people came to faith, the church never grew. He was also chaplain to a number of shops, to the local university, and to a branch of Age Concern – a "low point" was the failure of the church to own his chaplaincy work. At the same time he sought to engage in an ambitious redevelopment of the church premises, but things went 'pear-shaped' and with his blessing the church terminated his employment.

His toughest ministry was his retirement pastorate, where the local vicar banned him from the church school and where some members left the church because of his outward-facing ministry. This was a period when there were "good times, but also difficult times too".

Now in his second retirement, he misses people. He misses too "the visionary side of the ministry – discovering what is possible, and then seeking to make it a reality". However, the most difficult aspect of retirement is his wife's health – she needs full time care, and so, after fifty seven years of marriage, Leslie is living the life of a bachelor again.

As a result of some shrewd financial moves, Leslie had made some considerable savings. However, now he has to find £1,100 per week for nursing home charges. Nonetheless, he says "I am comfortable".

Leslie is a very positive person, even when now life is very challenging. He says he is "very happy" in the church, and finds the church "very supportive". Indeed, he feels "very much part of the church". Yet in my judgement the church has been anything but supportive. He says that he has "more than a few" friends in the church, but this 'friendliness' seems skin-deep. The two ministers have visited him, but nobody else from the church has. He leads two home groups, but no member has invited him for a meal. What is true of the church is true of people outside the church. Last Christmas he invited all his neighbours to drop by – but apart from one person, nobody did.

Not surprisingly, he notes that "retirement has proved to be a lonely experience".

His greatest need is "the need to be used". A church member for less than a year, he is already a deacon. Even although he is almost eighty, he is preaching in local churches and is looking for opportunities to get involved in the association. He is a real Caleb!

I came away from his home full of admiration for Leslie, but sad for him too.

Paul

Paul's call to ministry came through a sermon on Jeremiah preached by my father. At the time Paul was in his late teens and had already tried his hand at two or three jobs. He immediately went to Bible college, but at the end of the course was turned down by the area ministerial recognition committee. Paul, however, persevered, and with the help of the area superintendent found himself in charge of a small Baptist church on a tough council estate where there was no manse and a 'stipend' of £7 per week. For the next three years Paul was a 'bi-vocational' minister. travelling a twenty-mile round trip three days a week to support his wife and first child – and working in the church all the other hours of the week. The church grew rapidly – helped not least by the arrival in the first six months of four other young couples keen to serve the Lord. It was hard work – not least having to produce two sermons a week and a weekly Bible study in the midst of everything else.

After six or so years – which included a year at a Baptist college and gaining formal accreditation – Paul moved on to an even more challenging assignment, where twelve church members were "a constant potential for tension and creating difficult issues". The deacons were well-meaning but weak, and church meetings were a nightmare. Nonetheless Paul had the courage and strength to challenge the power-brokers, and change became the order of the day. Over the ten years the church flourished and young people abounded – with around a dozen baptisms every year.

In his third ministry lasting over twenty years Paul had the joy of seeing a medium-sized multi-cultural church with one minister grow into a very large church with a team of three ministers, five worship groups, and two part-time pastoral workers, engaged in a wide range of service, including a five-day-a-week pre-school and several luncheon clubs. Yet in spite of all the positives, there were low times too – not least the suicide of an assistant minister. Strangely, throughout almost all of his time there he had no effective church secretary – most of the administration load fell on him. Not surprisingly when Paul retired he experienced 'joy' and 'relief' – he was free at least of all that admin! Retirement for Paul has meant learning to live again, rather than be "run ragged". For him an important part of retirement is 'play' – "yes, yes, yes" he wrote.

As he looked back he said: "I count it a great privilege to have been called into the ministry and have been stretched and grown as a person through my experience of being in ministry. I do not feel I have emerged from ministry unscathed but rather honourably wounded as part of the price one pays of doing a job that involves dealing with difficult situations and people, along with making visionary decisions others may challenge but are right to make if the church is to develop in the future." Unfortunately, his two children paid the price of being 'children of the manse' and are no longer to be found in a church.

Financially more comfortable than many retired ministers, Paul attributes this to his not being in the Baptist pension scheme! He and his wife's combined income is under £40,000, and he says they "have no money problems".

Paul and his wife are involved in their local Baptist church where they have many 'friends' (acquaintances?). However, Paul is unhappy in the church: in spite of his offers of help, he feels ignored – the church is willing for him to preach, but fail to see that they can gain from his experience. Perhaps related to this is that he has found it difficult coming to terms with the loss of status in retirement. "I'm both challenged and amused by this experience, which I thought would not be an issue for me who did not count ministry as a kind of status symbol".

Paul no longer attends the church meeting and feels "very much on the edge". On a Sunday he is "content to be an ordinary 'punter' in the pew – except when the preacher produces an essay to be read – "What has happened to the old Baptist art of preaching in a flowing style, engaging with the congregation as one does so?" he asks.

Paul has a passion for "helping men to relate to church". He has set up a golf club for Christian men and their friends, and is also involved in various church men's groups. Another passion is gardening, which gives him many opportunities for conversations with people passing by. Paul and his wife have worked hard on taking the initiative to build relationships with many of the neighbours in their street.

I found it interesting that although in the first years of his retirement Paul was very involved in mentoring young ministers, he himself has never seen the need for a mentor in his retirement.

Like many of his peers, Paul's relationship with the Baptist Union and its regional ministry is non-existent. He has never had "a pastoral visit or a personal letter or a phone call" from his regional minister. When asked, "are you content with the support your currently receive", he replied "What support?" It is only because of the retired ministers' group to which he belongs, that he still feels "part of the wider Baptist family". Even then, his retired ministers' group is not ideal – too much time is spent reminiscing on the past, rather than building supportive relationships for the present. Although he is very much an outgoing character, ministry, he says, can be "a lonely road". Paul seems to have only one ministerial 'buddy' with whom he remains in touch.

I came away thinking, "I would have enjoyed being one of his members – he would have stimulated me".

Robin

Robin was a banker for ten years before training for the ministry – every now and again his wife wishes he had remained in the bank, where the prospects were bright and a good pension was guaranteed. As it is, they are "just managing" on a pension of £14,000.

Robin served for almost thirty years in ministry. His first pastorate was in Scotland – when he arrived congregations numbered around 30-40, but by the time he left they had risen to around 50-60. There was much spiritual growth too. However, after seven years Robin had to resign as a result of bullying– and all his deacons resigned too in solidarity with him. As he discovered to his cost, this church had a history of abusing pastors – two of the three previous pastors had left the ministry altogether, with a third having to seek pastures new.

After a difficult five-month period of unemployment, Robin was called to a church with over one hundred members in the Midlands. It proved a fruitful twelve years, characterised both by numerical and spiritual growth, but one deacon took against him and threatened to call a vote of non-confidence. For the sake of the unity of the church, Robin agreed to seek to move – but found it difficult to find another church. Rather than fight his corner at the church meeting, Robin took the course of encouraging his supporters to vote for his dismissal, which then made him eligible for benefits!

It was only after eighteen months of unemployment that Robin was called to his third and final church. Those nine years were happy years of ministry – so much so that the church wanted Robin to delay his retirement, but after all he had gone through Robin decided he had had enough.

The pain of ministry is still with Robin – and with his wife, who following all the difficulties for two years had to take anti-depressants. As Robin said. "we were treated worse by Christians than by unbelievers". Not surprisingly, when he retired, his emotions were a mixture of 'joy' ("I've finished") and 'relief' ("it's all over!"). In spite of everything Robin says that "for the most part ministry was rewarding, but there were tough times", and if he had the opportunity to begin life again, he would still want to be a Baptist minister – and his wife agrees!

Retirement has not been easy. The town to which they moved does not have a church in membership with the Baptist Union, and so he and his wife joined a 'Grace' Baptist church which subsequently joined the FIEC. He feels like "an ecclesiological alien" there, and not surprisingly feels "ignored" and is "treated with suspicion". He has no close church friends. Although his wife is fairly involved, he is less so, and spends much of his time at home reading voraciously. He reads through the Bible at least annually. This past year, influenced by two monastic communities, he divided the day into seven 'offices', and reads a chapter of the Bible at 6 am, 9 am, 10.30 am, 12 noon, 3 pm and 5.30 pm.

Robin "no longer" feels "part of the wider family" – he "feels forgotten by the Baptist family". He twice wrote to the local regional minister, but never received a reply – he even wrote to the regional minister's secretary to ensure that his letters had been received, but again received no reply. Like other retired ministers in his association he received a questionnaire asking whether he would be willing to preach in churches in the association or serve as a moderator. Robin, whose passion is preaching, filled in the questionnaire offering his service – but like many others, he heard no more.

It would mean a lot to him if his past ministry could at least be recognised by the wider Baptist Union. He commented on how newly accredited ministers are welcomed by the President at the annual Baptist Assembly – but then the next time a minister's name is mentioned at the Assembly, is after their death. He wondered whether ministers on retirement could receive a formal thank-you and a handshake at the following Assembly.

Retirement for Robin "has led to a restriction in life" and has "proved a lonely experience".

Roger

A former primary school teacher, over the years Roger has had three churches.

At the age of twenty-three he became a student pastor of a small church in a rough urban area – only in this way could he have enough money to survive.

After college he moved to a church where, apart from one young couple, all 120 members were elderly. In his six years he buried half his members, but the membership remained roughly the same thanks to all the young people and young families who joined. Although he felt he needed to close down the Brigades and shut a small struggling 'mission' associated with the church, nonetheless it was a time with no real difficulties. Rather it was a time of church 'regeneration' when many came to faith.

Much more challenging and demanding was his third church, where he stayed for twenty-five years. Roger was the church's first minister. When he arrived, the church had some 40 members – when he left there were 200 members and perhaps a further 300 people on the fringe. He experienced a time of "mini-revival" as whole families came to faith – "we sensed a move of God in our community". In that time the church went through four different "manifestations of church". Under his leadership the church acquired and renovated a large community centre. He says he never had a difficult church meeting – but there were many difficult people, some with massive pastoral needs. Although there were five paid members of staff, Roger was the only pastor. As a result, toward the end of his ministry he became exhausted – "the cracks began to show" – and he retired at the age of 57.

Roger was able to retire early because he already had his own house – there had been no manse in his third church. With the help of a legacy and a gift from relatives, together with a degree of financial astuteness, he and his wife's combined income now is under £40,000.

Roger is a bundle of energy. A hard-working magistrate who oversees the recruitment and interviewing of new magistrates as also dealing with disciplinary issues, he writes a good deal and is in demand as an after-dinner speaker. The best thing about retirement, he says, is "the freedom to actually say 'No' to something and not feel guilty". He takes off Wednesdays, so that he and his wife can have time together.

His local Baptist church is "fairly dead", and so he and his wife now worship in their local parish church. A strong evangelical church, there are plenty of activities for young families – however, Roger "along with the other over-fifties" feels currently ignored. They have made "a few friends" in the church, but as Roger admits, they are often away because of preaching or family commitments". Instead of mentoring younger ministers, Roger has mentored older ministers: currently he is helping a retired minister who struggles with the reality of retirement.

Roger did receive a visit from his regional minister – but only because he asked to see him. "It was a waste of time", said Roger. "Instead of listening, he talked about himself". Roger is "profoundly concerned that there is an enormous need in our retired ministers which is disregarded, and a resource in our retired ministers which is largely ignored". He went on: "I know that there are retired ministers who are a 'pain' in that they are always talking about 'the good old days'. However, there are large numbers of us feeling puzzled, ignored, and rankly undervalued". Not surprisingly, he feels "no longer part of the wider Baptist family".

Rowland

Rowland did national service (RAF) and worked in industry before starting to train for ministry at the age of twenty-four.

He is a 'battle-scared' older minister who in almost forty years of service had three tough ministries. In each of them he saw growth, but not one was easy. In his first ministry his colleague had a breakdown, and his predecessor committed suicide.

His second church was on a huge council estate where he enjoyed an "excellent children's ministry" – alas the church was always short of cash and for much of the time the church was stuck in a legal dispute.

His lowest point was in his third church when a small group in one of his churches tried to oust him – not surprisingly the 'in-fighting' took its toll on the church's outreach to the wider community. However, he looks back with fondness on his time as a pastor – and if given an opportunity would still want to be a Baptist minister. High points for him were meeting people, worship and teaching, visiting and caring for people, and working in the community. Rowland has clearly been a hard-working 'old-school' minister, much respected by his church members.

His and his wife's combined pensions come to less than £20,000, but they feel "comfortable". In his first eight years of retirement he supplemented his income as a taxi-driver. Rowland is grateful to rent a property from the RBMHS.

Retirement has not been easy. The minister of his local Baptist church refused to receive him and his wife into membership: "there is no place in this church for you", he said – did he feel 'threatened' by Rowland? This was a painful experience and Rowland has never found a permanent spiritual home in retirement - he tends to worship in a local Anglican church, where he has a good relationship with the vicar, but also worships at a local independent evangelical church. His wife, however, became joined the women's meeting at the Baptist church.

In his retirement he has continued to preach and lead Bible studies. He has found particular fulfilment in working as a volunteer for two mission agencies. For many years he has also been an active Rotarian. He works in a wide variety of community projects – amongst others he serves as a school governor and paints airplanes at Duxford. Along with preaching and leading worship, he says that his passions are family, airplanes, trains and buses.

An outgoing man with a great sense of humour, Rowland has lots of 'casual' friends (acquaintances) but no close friends. In the last six months no church person has invited him and his wife into their home.

In the last year or so his wife has become seriously ill, and he has had to become a carer. Although his wife spent many weeks in hospital, she received no visits from any Baptist minister – Rowland found this lack of care an upsetting experience. Fortunately, his children have been supportive.

Throughout his active ministry Rowland was highly committed both to the Baptist Union and to association life, but since retirement he has not had a pastoral visit or a personal letter or phone call from any regional minister. He now no longer feels part of the wider Baptist family. As he said, he would love to have some acknowledgement that "we still exist". The demise of the Baptist Directory and the omission of retired ministers from the Association handbook troubles him. He is sad that the association does not want to take advantage of all the experience retired Baptist ministers have to offer.

Sam

Sam left school at the age of fifteen to go into the family farming business – and when they married his wife had no idea that they would end up in ministry. However, she did know that Sam was considering the possibility of becoming an agricultural missionary, but when she began to have some health problems, the door to overseas mission shut. Then, much to Sam's surprise, God called him into ministry!

A relatively late entrant, Sam served just under twenty years in stipendiary ministry. Both his churches were challenging, and both churches were small and struggling. Sam ended up not just "sowing the seed and caring for people", but also caring for the buildings, serving as treasurer, and in one church also serving as church secretary. Sam was very much a 'Jack-of-all-trades'. He lists as his highlights baptisms and sharing as a pastor in significant events in the lives of others. The low points have been a sense of isolation, assertive deacons, marriages of church people breaking down. Reflecting on his experience of ministry, he said "there were good times, but there were difficult times too".

For family reasons Sam has stayed on in his last church and still feels "quite part of the church". He has developed a good relationship with his much younger successor. Although Sam at times plays the role of a mentor to him, he is quite clear that he is spiritually accountable to his minister.

By contrast with many Baptist ministers, Sam is comfortably off and together with his wife has a combined income of under £50,000. He was able to buy his present house because he had a house before he became a minister. His finances were helped by his wife having had for a period a well-paid job. However, Sam is amazingly generous. He gave a gift of £50,000 to his church to help it out of a difficulty – even although his only child, now in his twenties, will always need support. What's more, to save the church money, he works a good number of hours a week as the church's cleaner – he is also the treasurer of the church! But then, Sam says that the best thing he enjoys about retirement is that he can work "for love rather than pay".

Sam still misses being the minister of a church. Although relieved no longer to have the responsibility of leadership, he misses "the privilege of expressing my convictions relating to the gospel and discipleship".

Sam has a servant-heart and even in retirement is always getting his hands 'dirty' in his service of the church – and of others. I was therefore saddened to see that that in the last six months no church member has invited him and his wife into their home for a meal. Indeed, he says that he has only "a few" friends in the church. One of those friends is a retired Baptist minister, who has been very supportive to Sam.

In his retirement Sam has received no support from his local association or the wider Baptist Union – although typical of Sam, he expresses gratitude for his Baptist Union pension. He has not had any contact with any regional minister during the seven years of his retirement. Nonetheless because he was born into a Baptist home, was converted in a Baptist church, and is a convinced Baptist himself, Sam says he still feels "part of the wider Baptist family".

Sam is one of the most self-deprecating Baptist ministers I know – and yet I would honour him in the way in which he has lived out the 'ministry of the towel' (John 13).

Simon

After a brief spell as a trainee buyer, Simon began training for the ministry at the age of twenty-one, and served over forty years in stipendiary ministry. Of his six churches, his first was far and away the happiest: in the seven years the church grew from 19 to 109 members. His next church also experienced much growth and there were many baptisms, but his ministry was marked by tensions associated with charismatic renewal. His third church proved a disaster and lasted only five months – the church failed to provide reasonable accommodation for his family, and after a good deal of 'nastiness' Simon was given notice. In the process, the children suffered, with one of them attending four different schools during that period. Fortunately. Simon's next church proved a much more positive experience, including a great youth group for Simon's children – nonetheless "there were moments" of difficulty. Simon got on very well with his fifth church, until two female members of staff fell out with him: rather than allow their deteriorating relationships to split the church, Simon felt it best to resign. After all the pain, his final church proved a healing experience and enabled Simon to end ministry well. All in all, "there were good times, but there were difficult times too".

I do not understand all the difficulties which Simon encountered, but from my experience of Simon I know he is not a man who by nature finds it difficult to get on with people. He is a very sociable and easy-going person. True, he admits there were times when he made mistakes, but this is not the reason why so much went 'pear-shaped' in his ministry. In the light of all the ups and downs they experienced, Simon's wife would not be keen to be a minister's wife again – she has had enough of the pain.

They are now happily settled in a new home – the purchase of which was made possible by another family member coming to live with them. With a combined income of under £30,000 Sam and his wife say they "enough to live in".

The first year or so of retirement was not easy. Simon found it difficult settling down as an ordinary church member. For the first four months they went to one lively church, but never received a welcome – none of the leaders seemed to want them. Eventually, they joined another Baptist church – but even there Simon felt kept on the periphery. At this point Simon decided to return to ministry on a part-time basis.

Unfortunately, his part-time pastorate does not really bring him the sense of fulfilment he looked for. True, after a devastating experience of a previous pastor, who almost destroyed the church, the congregation has begun to grow – from four to sometimes twenty people on a Sunday. But neither Simon or his wife have been able to make friends in the church – and nobody from the church has invited them into their homes for a meal. I wonder how long Simon will stay there. Maybe he needs to find interests beyond the local church.

Simon and his wife were very involved in denominational life prior to Simon's retirement, but they now feel unsupported by the present regional ministers. When asked, "how much do you feel part of the wider Baptist family", Simon could only say, "I feel neither one thing nor another". Simon is still at the stage of retirement when he feels he has much to give to Baptist church life – but his offer of help appears to be unwanted.

Tom

Tom spent fourteen years as a ladies' hairdresser, which he maintains was a great preparation for ministry. His call to ministry was gradual – before going to college he ran a Christian conference centre for five years, and served as a lay pastor for a further three years.

His first church was difficult. A large village church dominated by one family, it was extraordinarily inward-looking. Church meetings proved "horrible" as, without success, he sought to bring about change. Although the church was sorry to see him go, after three years he felt he had no other option but to move on.

His second church had its difficulties but was a much more positive experience – so much so that he stayed for twenty-eight years. There were many conversions and baptisms, and new church premises were built. Under his ministry the church became a thriving 'community' church. At one stage the work amongst children and young people was so successful, that there were 'waiting lists' – although if children and young people came on a Sunday, they were fast-tracked into the mid-week programme. In spite of the evident blessing, ten years into his ministry two deacons asked him to leave – fortunately the church rallied round, but the way in which his position was challenged proved a very low point.

As he looks back on his ministry, he says that "for the most part it was rewarding, but there were tough times". Had he the opportunity, he would want to be a Baptist minister again – but for him "a very strong call" is vital to surviving in ministry.

His two key emotions in the first months of retirement were 'joy' and 'relief'. The joy came through having "gone through the tape". His mission was accomplished. Unlike many of his peers, who had not survived in ministry, he had "made it". He also experienced a great sense of 'relief': although he missed the people, he was delighted that the "pressures" of ministry were over – he was a free man at last!

Tom and his wife celebrated their new-found freedom by taking "a gap year" before settling down into retirement. The gap year included six months of touring the country by caravan.

For family reasons they still live in the same area as their last church. They have moved from a large four-bedroomed church manse into a much smaller two-bedroomed house bought for them by the RBMHS – into which they had to plough some money of their own. Financially, with a combined income of under £30,000, they "have enough to live on".

Tom and his wife now worship at their local parish church, where the rector has made them warmly welcome. He finds the difference between the parish church and a Baptist church is "refreshing" – he has come to enjoy the Anglican liturgy. The rector sees Tom as a valuable pastoral resource, and so Tom preaches in the church regularly and leads a home group. There are seven or eight retired Anglican ministers in the church: Tom appreciates the opportunity to join them for a monthly study morning led by a retired college tutor. Tom also belongs to a group for retired Baptist ministers which meets every two months, and feels well supported there.

Tom and his wife are part of various friendship circles: there are two couples from their last church with whom they are close; they have made "a few" friends in the parish church; and as a result of having got two dogs are developing many friends in the dog-walking community.

Vic

Vic left school at the age of fifteen with no qualifications to become a cabinet-maker – now in retirement he enjoys working with wood again. Responding to God's call, he went to a Baptist college and then served for almost forty years in stipendiary ministry.

The first eleven happy years were spent in an estate church which grew from 12 to 82 members, and where over 300 children belonged to the Sunday School. God really blessed his ministry. To the amazement of all his friends he then moved to a town-centre church which was threatened with closure: the congregation was elderly and the buildings were in a terrible state. The first five years in his second church were "awful" – the area superintendent suggested a move, but Vic felt called and persevered. By the end of his ministry he left a church in fine fettle. As he looks back upon his ministry, he says: "For the most part it was rewarding, but there were tough times". High points included "baptizing many new members into Christ and his church, preaching each Sunday, and learning from older experienced Christians". Low points included a former minister who stayed on in membership and who made things difficult for him.

When Vic retired in 1999, his chief emotion was "joy" – he felt deeply grateful to God for blessing him in ministry and enabling him to accomplish his mission. He said, "I loved the work of the ministry and would do it all again"

In many ways retirement has been a good experience for Vic. Thanks to his wife having had a well-paid job, housing was not an issue - he continues to live in a large and comfortable bungalow. With an income of under £30,000 he has "no money problems".

Over the years he has enjoyed pursuing a wide range of interests and hobbies, and has made many new friends outside the church as a result. He maintains a lively mind: in the last three months he read two books by Tom Wright, as well as some non-theological books. Vic is an engaging and positive person, and I was impressed by his love for his Lord.

His experience of church in retirement has not been so good. He and his wife joined a Baptist church some four miles away, believing it to offer opportunities for further service – and even now in his eighties he still runs a Bible study group. However, were he not running the group, he would have moved to a local Anglican church – at the moment he is "unhappy" in the church and "just hanging on". According to Vic, his minister sees his role on a Sunday to be "a stand-up comic" and "never visits" during the week. Vic speaks of the church members being "very supportive", but in the last six months only one member has invited him into their home. Fortunately, his three married daughters, all of whom are relatively local, take him out and see to his needs.

His greatest sadness in retirement is his non-existent relationship with the wider Baptist family. No regional minister has ever been in touch with him – not even when his wife died. As he wrote on his questionnaire, "I would like regional ministers to know that I exist". He says "I no longer feel part of the wider Baptist family".

William

With degrees in classics and theology, William is a thoughtful man. After teaching for twelve years – including a spell in Africa – he served twenty-five years in Baptist ministry.

William had three challenging churches. His happiest and seemingly most fruitful ministry was his first church, where over twelve years he had the joy of baptizing more than eighty people – but the first few years were tough, not least when he felt it right to get back to basics by shutting down all the church activities apart from the Sunday services and the mid-week Bible study!

His second church was a nightmare, where a small group of gifted elders bullied him, failed to provide him and his family with a manse, and then in the end sacked him. During this extraordinarily difficult time, William began to suffer from depression. The pain of that ministry is still real – although William says he has forgiven his abusers, he cannot forget those years.

His final ministry was by the sea. The setting was idyllic, but the church was in a time-warp, and there again there were difficulties: the organist refused to co-operate and one leader did his best to oust William.

As William looks back, he says "there were good times, but there were difficult times". William regrets the extent to which his children were affected by "times of extreme tension". Not surprisingly William's first months of retirement were characterised by a sense of relief. For him the best thing about retirement is "freedom from pressures of ministry".

In his retirement William was fortunate to be able to purchase a house of his own – in part because he had a house before he became a minister, but also because he had a legacy and a working wife. They now have a lovely home and are well pleased to be where they are. With a combined income of under £30,000, they have "enough to live on".

He has not been so fortunate in his relationship with his present church. There he feels unhappy; he has no support, but instead is treated like any other retired person. He feels very

47

much on the edge. This is strange, because William and his wife are a delightful couple, whom I would have loved to have as members of my church. William has offered to help with preaching and with other pastoral duties, but his offer was turned down by both the past and present ministers – perhaps because of their own insecurity, but also perhaps because they fail to see that retired ministers have anything to offer. Although William has sought to make relationships within the church, they have few friends – and in the past six months only one couple have invited him and his wife into their home for a meal. William has found a greater depth of friendship outside the church – not least arising from his work in the community as a teacher of English as a foreign language.

As for the wider Baptist family, William feels "neither one thing or another". He has had no contact from any regional minister. Thankfully he is happy in the retired ministers' group to which he belongs.

SECTION TWO: THE RETIREMENT EXPERIENCE:

AN ANALYSIS OF THE DATA

1.   GENERAL INFORMATION

Gender

Some 94% of those participating in this survey were male. This imbalance reflects the fact that although the Baptist Union of Great Britain has had women ministers for over eighty years, the proportion remains relatively low. [14] There has been an increase in recent years – currently some 13% of ministers are women, while of those students training for accredited ministry some 30% are women; but this increase has yet to reflect itself in the figures of the retired.

Marital status

Some 79% of respondents were married, with a further 13% widowed. Some 5% had never married, while the one respondent who had been divorced commented: "divorced prior to ordination, but then remarried for 31+ years".

Age

Although the selection of respondents to the survey was quite random, nonetheless there was a good representative spread of ages. For instance the proportion of respondents 75 years and

---

[14] In 1918 Edith Gates became minister of Little Tew and Cleveley, Oxfordshire, and in 1922 was enrolled as a probationer by the Ministerial Recognition Committee. In 1924 Violet Hedger became the first female student to complete her studies at a Baptist college (Regent's Park College) but did not get a church until 1926 when she went to Littleover in Derbyshire.

over was exactly the same as the proportion of ministers in the Baptist Pension scheme 75 years and over: viz. 36%.

How old were you when you retired?

In view of the current tendency in the wider world to encourage people to consider delaying retirement, it was interesting to discover that over half of the respondents retired at the traditional age of 65. Only six retired later – with just two delaying retirement at 70.

How long have you been retired from stipendiary ministry?

Just over half (56%) had been retired for less than ten years, with 20% having retired in the last five years. Just over a third (36%) had been retired between 11 and 20 years. Only around 4% had been retired for more than 21 years – in addition there was one non-stipendiary ministry who had been retired 16-20 years.

Paid employment since retirement

Just over a quarter (26%) of respondents took up paid employment after retirement. Three were part-time pastors; one a part-time hospital chaplain, another a part-time university chaplain; and one an assistant camp-side warden in the context of an evangelistic project. Others had been a college tutor, a mentor, a taxi driver, a translator, and a worker in IT support.

2. PAST EXPERIENCE OF MINISTRY

How many years did you serve in stipendiary ministry?

Most of the respondents in this survey had served for many years. Almost a third (32%) had served for less than 30 years, while well over half (62%) had served for more than 31 years. The table reflects that in the mid to late twentieth century most students training for ministry in Baptist colleges were under 25 – late entrants were rare.

Most respondents spent their active ministry in local church life, but some had spent part of their ministerial service in 'trans-local' ministry: for example, one had been in Christian TV for a time; another had for eight years combined ministry with full-time teaching; one had been a superintendent and regional minister; two had been association general secretaries; two had served for short terms in Baptist House; three had been chaplains; five had served overseas as missionaries and/or in a missionary training college.

Did you have a good experience of ministry?

Almost three-quarters (72%) replied: "For the most part it was rewarding, but there were tough times". Only one said without qualification: "I have had a wonderful time" – however, the questionnaire revealed that he had known tough times too. A quarter (25%) however, had known exceedingly tough times and reported "there were good times, but there were difficult times too". Only one said: "It was tough and often unrewarding" – and none said, in terms of their experience of ministry as a whole "It was very tough – my ministry was often rejected". [15]

It needs to be borne in mind that this survey was conducted amongst the 'survivors' in ministry. In 2001, for instance, an analysis of Baptist ministers revealed that over a fifty-year period (1946-1995) half of those enrolled onto the list of Accredited Ministers of the Baptist Union of Great Britain did not retire on it.[16] Although the fall-out has decreased substantially, not least through the way in which 'newly

---

[15] In *Power for God's Sake*, 103 I reported that Baptist ministers in particular felt there had been times when they had been unjustly treated: 81% mentioned unjust treatment by individual members; 39% unjust treatment by deacons/elders; and 16% unjust treatment by church staff.

[16] See Nigel Coles, 'Ministry Fallout: Can we afford it? Can we prevent it?', *Ministry Today* 24 (Spring 2002) 22-28. See also Paul Beasley-Murray, 'The challenge of ministry today' in *Living out the call:1. Living for God's Glory* 16-18.

accredited ministers' are now cared for, there are still those who do not 'survive' the rigours of ministry.

What were the high and low points?

The high points inevitably varied. However, repeatedly respondents commented on

- seeing people young and old coming to faith
- the joy of baptising new Christians
- experiencing church growth
- leading worship
- presiding at the Lord's Table
- preaching every Sunday to the same people
- pastoral visiting and care
- being part of people's lives
- taking dedications, weddings and funerals
- developing church premises
- working with others

The low points were less varied: one mentioned "having to confront racism and sexism in otherwise really lovely people", four mentioned a wife's illness; two wrote of difficulties arising from safeguarding issues; one drew attention of "lack of finance", and another to "lack of resources.

However, overwhelmingly the issues raised dealt with politics and power struggles; conflict and dissension; manipulation, criticism, gossip, back-biting; resistance to change and resulting opposition; bullying and aggression from deacons; breakdown of relationships with other members of a staff team; misunderstanding and rejection. As one retired minister wrote ruefully, Baptists are "a fissiparous, argumentative lot!" As a result some ministers felt they had to resign – others were sacked; yet others suffered clinical depression and had to take time off work.

If you had an opportunity to begin life again, would you want to be a minister?

In view of the challenging nature of ministry today, the respondents were amazingly positive. Over half (57%) said without qualification that if they had an opportunity, they would want to be a minister again. "200%" replied one respondent. Interestingly all three respondents who had come late into ministry who were particularly enthusiastic: "the best thing I have ever done"; "I know of nothing else like it"; "I should have answered the call earlier in my life". Another replied with an understanding *caveat*: "Yes – but with the wisdom I have gained over the years, and not as a novice".

In so far as the call of God is at the heart of ministry, [17] it was not surprising that almost a fifth (18%) added "only if God called". Responses included: "the sense of call is vital"; "I am not sure that I ever 'wanted' to be a Baptist minister, it was more that I was willing if God called me". One of the older respondents wrote: "I don't think I would choose the ministry of the church as a profession, and I'm sure few would; we would agree that there has to be a sense of call and of imperative.... I have to stop myself looking back too often to the earliest days, how we young men were sent out from college to the hardest of situations with little or not support.... in those years a lot of my contemporaries left the ministry, one friend committing suicide stuck in a fenland situation."

A quarter (25%) were not sure whether they wanted to enter ministry again: "a very difficult question to answer"; "probably yes, though I might approach the whole thing differently"; "yes, but a career in politics or the law often seemed more attractive". Almost a fifth (18%) had reservations about serving within the Baptist Union as it is today: "present-day Baptist don't seem to be what they were"; "Baptists have lost their way"; "it would depend on the churchmanship of the Baptist church"; "that would depend on how 'Baptist church was and is defined, and how it works – I was wholeheartedly supportive of Baptist

---

[17] See Paul Beasley-Murray, *Living out the Call: 1. Living for God's Glory*, 'A call to ministry' 8-11.

principles as they were understood and practised and I committed myself to ministry in the Baptist context".

Significantly, not one respondent replied with a blunt "No"! [18]

Would your spouse want to be married to a Baptist minister?

Yes:	28
Yes, if called	5
Probably not	5
Unsure	5
No	3
Married only for love	3
Unmarried	3
Widowed	3
She would want to be a minister	1
Too personal	1

Almost two thirds (62%) of spouses appear to have a positive view of ministry. Over half felt their spouses would want to be married to a Baptist minister ("provided it was the same one", several commented!), a number would only do so if there were a sense of call – "I wouldn't choose to do it", said one. While one wife said, if she had the opportunity, she would love to be a Baptist minister herself.

By contrast 25% of spouses had a less positive view of ministry. Some respondents replied that they were "unsure" while others thought "probably not". "My spouse would share my own

---

[18] See the concluding section of Paul Beasley-Murray, *This is my Story: a story of life, faith and ministry*: "I thank God for the privilege of having been a pastor. It is undoubtedly the most wonderful calling in the world. I thank God for so much happiness and fulfilment in ministry; I thank God even for the tough times, because they have brought about a depth and maturity which otherwise I would not have had."

ambivalence in respect of the experience of having been in Baptist ministry", said one; "my wife found, at times, the expectations hard", said another; "it was a stressful experience", said a third.

Almost 6% would definitely not wish to be married to a Baptist minister: "The expectations were overwhelming"; "Forty years of ministerial life has taken its toll and while my wife still has a strong firm faith in God she does not want to be involved in a Baptist church, or any church for that matter". One spouse made the following comments: "the church takes over your whole life"; "the pay and conditions were not good"; "the children lost out when the church came first"; "I saw my husband suffer too much". [19] Ministry can be tough for spouses.

Almost 6% of spouses married only for love – "and would do so again, whatever their husband's job".

Of those who were widowed, half made no reply, but the other half responded positively on behalf of their late wives!

Would your children want to be involved again in church life?

Yes:	18
Some/one would, the other/s not:	8
Unsure	14
No	5
No children	8

A third (34%) gave an unequivocal 'Yes'. 15% said that some of their children had had had a very positive experience of church, while others of their children had experienced "a complete turn-off in relation to church". One respondent commented: "one of our children turned away from church, but not from Jesus

---

[19] See *Power for God's Sake* 104: 76% of ministers claimed that their spouses had experienced "hurt" as a result of their being in ministry; while 55% of ministers said that their spouse/family had experienced "abuse" as a result of their being ministry.

Christ, because of the mismatch between faith and Christian behaviour towards me in some leading Christians at a key time in his life".

Over a quarter (26%) were unsure: "Who knows? Sadly they are not involved with church now, but they do have good memories of some of the things they did as part of a church".

Almost 10% said their children would definitely not want to be involved in church life – "they were badly burnt" said one respondent; another regretted the extent to which his children were affected by times of extreme tension"; another mentioned the unhelpful expectations that some church members have of ministers' children.

Ministry can be tough for the 'children of the Manse'.[20]

3. TRANSITION TO RETIREMENT

Did you receive helpful advice?

While over half (55%) were very positive, a number were critical of the Baptist Union retirement course, not least because there were times when the leader of the course had no experience of ministry. Just over a third (36%) had received helpful advice from other retired people; and 6% said they had received helpful advice from a regional minister or a financial advisor.

13% mentioned they had received help from books on retirement, but none specified the books they had read. In conversation one minister mentioned *Finishing Our Course*

---

[20] See Paul Beasley-Murray, *This is my story*: "There are great advantages to being a PK [Pastor's Kid] to develop self-confidence and social skills. It's not surprising that many PKs do well in life and contribute much to society. But life is not always easy for PKs. There are times when churches abuse their pastors, and in so doing they abuse the children too. I fear for leaders of such churches when they have to stand at the last judgment and give an account of the way in which they treated the 'little ones' in their care (see Matt 18:6). Sadly, many PKs have been driven out of the church."

with Joy by Jim Packer; [21] another *A Good Old Age* by Derek Prime; [22] yet another *The Highway Code for Retirement* by David Winter. [23]

However, almost two-fifths (38%) said they had received no helpful advice.

Statistically, it is important to note that some received advice from more than one source

What weren't you prepared for and how did you make the adjustments?

26% said they were "well prepared for retirement" and "found the adjustment very easy". Others did not find the transition so easy.

A sense of loss. Several mentioned how difficult they found "the loss of role in church life" and the "loss of the close relationship with the congregation". "It was like a bereavement", said one minister.

A sense of being on the edge. Several mentioned that churches are not always good at welcoming retired ministers. "The hardest thing in our new church was coffee-time when we had to try and make conversation with people we did not know", wrote one respondent. "Getting to know people was harder than we thought". There was a resulting "loneliness" said another.

An inability to be an ordinary church member. "I was ready to lay down the responsibilities as a pastor, as the last two years had been tough and I was exhausted; I didn't think beyond that. What I wasn't prepared for was how hard it is to feel at home in a local church as an 'ordinary church member'.

---

[21] Jim Packer, *Finishing our Course with Joy: Ageing with Hope* (IVP, Nottingham 2014).

[22] Derek Prime, *A Good Old Age: An A to Z of loving and following the Lord Jesus in later years* (10 Publishing, Leyland, Lancashire 2017).

[23] David Winter, *The Highway Code for Retirement* (CWR, Farnham, Surrey 2012).

I'm coming to the conclusion that it's impossible. Retirement from ministry is not like other retirements; you're still expected to be involved in what was your job/life (albeit in a different context."

An empty diary: I had "so much time on my hands", said one. "The phone stopped ringing", said another.

Disappointment that church leaders did not want to benefit from their experience. Two mentioned how in an inter-regnum their church was happy to invite them to preach, but not to ask for help in the search for a new minister: "my advice was never sought, my experience though offered was never tapped".

The adjustment remains ongoing, said one retired minister: "I have to still continue to make adjustments it brought, in the mind and the emotions, because it deeply affects the sense of personal identity – even with a solid sense of who I am in Christ".

If you were speaking to a group of younger pastors, what would be your advice to help them prepare for retirement?

The advice varied, but included:

Start early planning: "five to ten years ahead", said one minister.

Prepare financially: "start making financial plans". "get the finances sorted out"; make sure you have a good pension scheme"; "make sure you have made adequate financial provision for your spouse if widowed". One said: "Start thinking and planning financially from when you leave college. If at all possible, try to buy a small property to rent out and grow this asset over time".

Develop interests and hobbies: "look for a hobby or interest that can be developed into retirement"; "develop interests and hobbies"; "take up worthwhile pastimes or sports.

Find a new church before a new home: "I am surprised by some of the moves fellow Christians make on retirement, seemingly taking little account of their spiritual needs and service"; "find a church which has a minister, so that you can receive ministry, rather than needing to minister".

Accept that church will never be the same: "Don't expect your relationship to a church to ever be the same again; don't feel guilty about now wanting to be part of a church".

Develop a strategy for future service: "Think ahead what you would wish to continue in ministry (at a different pace and level) and take steps to seize opportunities – if people don't come to you, be prepared to take the initiative of offering particular areas of ministry". Another advised: "Make sure you have a reason for getting out of bed". Other advice included "retirement means ceasing stipendiary employment and finding new ways of serving God"; "try to keep up the aspects of ministry you enjoy, and feel free to drop those you don't".

Make sure you know who you are: "Don't define yourself by what you do"

What emotions did you feel in the first months of retirement?

Relief was the overwhelming emotion, mentioned by just over half (51%) the respondents. Thank God, the pressures of ministry had ceased – "no more meetings", wrote one minister; "no longer having to bear the responsibility", said another.

Joy was mentioned by two-fifths (42%). This was for the most part not defined, but several mentioned the joy of "being able to spend more time with my wife"; another "not having to go out to meetings every night"; yet another, the joy of "mission completed"; and another "the sense of a new beginning".

Loneliness was mentioned by 15%. "I missed people", said one. Another mentioned loneliness in the context of not being part of a ministers' group: "Who is there to help me with all the theological questions that have come to me now that I have more time to reflect on what I really believe?"

Frustration was experienced by over 7% - this related particularly to issues surrounding housing.

Depression or "deep sadness" was highlighted over 11%. In part this related to "disappointment of being disposed of" and was symptomatic of the loss of role. [24] Perhaps for some there was also the sadness of not being able to complete all that they felt God had called them to do? [25] Two other emotions, unmentioned by the respondents, but related to depression and sadness, are guilt and regret. A former Baptist Union 'head of ministry', Norman Jones, wrote movingly of looking back on his ministry and feeling he had misused his time in ministry: "The diary was the master, good works the order of the day, everything else secondary; selfishly sacrificed to one's own ego, which demanded that you 'give and not count the cost".[26]

Note that some experienced more than one emotion!

---

[24] David Baker, 'Adjustments in retirement', *BMJ* 293 (January 2006) 26 wrote: "Emotionally I see retirement from full-time Ministry like a bereavement; it is the loss of a role I have been in for a number of years. Some of the same symptoms are there: numbness, denial, anger/depression, various questionings about where we are going; then eventually comes real acceptance. I say 'real' because I have had times over the past years when I thought I had accepted it but then realised I had not done so".

[25] Paul Tournier, *Learning to Grow Old* (SCM, London 1960) 169-170 maintained that 'acceptance of unfulfilment' is one of the great problems of the retired. He went on: "Of God alone can the Bible say (Gen 2.1) that on the evening of the sixth day of retirement he had completed his work".

[26] Norman B. Jones, 'One man's retirement', *Fraternal* 190 (January 1980) 19-20, who continued: "So much has been lost and rarely for the causes I set out to serve. How much richer that service would have been if I had been a richer person, if I had observed nature in more detail, if I had developed a deeper understanding of literature and music, and above all, if I had observed in greater detail the surprising development of my family. So much time has been spent in knowing people. So little in knowing them. So much time in serving God, and so little to become sensitive to his presence. Yes, there is much to regret about the past, as there is also forgiveness for it."

Do you still miss being the minister of a church?

Almost half (49%) said they still missed being a pastor. "I miss Christmas, Easter, baptisms and people – had I the energy I would start all over again"; "I miss the close relationship with people and the opportunity for consistent preaching".

Almost 6% mentioned how much they missed leading a church – "I miss being at the centre of things, being the driver of vision and seeing it unfold, being respected for the position one holds as the minister of the church and being listened to, being at the centre of things such as special events. Taking charge of events and moving them forward rather than sitting on the side-lines and wishing someone would get a grip of things." Similarly another wrote: "I miss the visionary side of ministry – discovering what is possible, and then seeking to make it a reality". Or as one said 'tongue in cheek': "I miss being in a church where everything is done 'my way'".

On the other hand, one respondent replied: "Yes – but not the deacons and church meetings". Another wrote "I miss it, but at 92 I am content with helping at Bible studies and house groups".

A smaller but substantial number (38%) said no: "I have done my time"; "regular opportunities to be involved in a local church and preach from time are enough for me".

4% missed being the minister "a little". "When I perceive the existing leadership not doing it very well!", said one. Or as another wrote: "Only for short periods…. I miss people I was close to; I miss having a role sometimes; I miss knowing the congregation in a way a pastor does".

9% said both "yes and no". For instance, one wrote of missing "being part of a local church in which your contribution is known" as also "a clear sense of belonging".

4.   HOUSING ISSUES

For young ministers a church house is often an undoubted perk. At a stage when most of their peers are in small homes, they may well have a four if not five-bed-roomed house, with often one or two receptions rooms. However, when retirement comes, there are huge problems for many ministers because they do not have a house. Some therefore argue that manses and the system of tied housing should be abolished, and that ministers should be paid a housing allowance to enable them to own their own home. The fact is that the current system of tied housing always favours the church, and not the minister – for while the church continually profits from rising house-prices, the minister continually loses out. There is, however, one strong argument in the provision of church manses: it facilitates the moving of ministers – particularly from lower-priced areas in the North to more expensive-priced areas in the South. Indeed, without a church manse, the provision of ministry in many parts of London would be well-nigh impossible.

It was because of the problem of housing that the Retired Baptist Ministers Housing Society was set up in 1974 to provide permanent homes with assured tenancies for accredited Baptist ministers who had served for a period of not normally less than fifteen years. Today the RBMHS owns over 250 properties. Although for some the house provided was not ideal, with one exception, all of the ministers I interviewed were grateful for the accommodation provided. They were grateful too for the relatively small monthly rent which is charged – the rent is calculated as 10% of a household's taxable income.

How difficult was the issue of housing for retirement?

Very difficult: 2

Difficult: 4

OK: 17

Easy: 11

Very easy: 19

It is gratifying to see that over half (57%) found the issue of housing "easy" or "very easy; while almost a third (32%) found the process "OK".

The few (almost 3%) who found the housing issue "very difficult" attributed their difficulties to the RBMHS: one said "the RBMHS did not have sufficient houses – hence our going into part-time ministry in a church that had a small manse"; another said that the process was "one of humiliation and of pain because the society is not able to fulfil its role in any meaningful way".

Of the almost 8% who found the process "difficult", 6% went on to live in RBMHS accommodation: the difficulty encountered by the latter was because of the 'ceiling price' the RBMHS has to put on the purchase price of a property. For if the Society does not have an available house in the area in which a retired minister wishes to live, then it is willing to seek to purchase a suitable house, subject to a ceiling price related to the cost of an average house in the UK: in 2018 this is £195,000. For ministers happy to live in parts of the country where housing is relatively cheap, this ceiling price provides few problems; however, in the more expensive parts of the South East can create real difficulty. True, it is possible for applicants to make a voluntary contribution and extend the limit of the Society's maximum purchase price by up to 25%, but not all ministers have such financial resources.

On the other hand, 4% of respondents gave the credit to the RBMHS for making the housing issue either "easy" or "very easy". On the positive side, too, a number in conversation with me talked of the security which the RMBHS has given them – as one said, even if I were to become a Buddhist, I would not be ejected![27]

---

[27] See also David Baker, 'Adjustments in retirement' 25: "Our new situation gives Pauline and I a sense of security and freedom as it is the first house we have lived in that is not tied to my work... We have a secure tenancy, and good support from the RBMHS".

In the individual interviews, a number mentioned the emotional difficulty of 'down-sizing'. What is not always appreciated is that most ministers, when they move at the point of their retirement, have to move to a smaller home, and in the process lose many of their possessions – including not just furniture but also many of their books. The latter loss can be quite heart-breaking!

How did you afford to buy your own home?

I received a legacy from parents/family members	17
My spouse made it possible	13
I had a house before I became a minister:	11
I was helped by my church	3
I had enough money to buy my own house	4
I had enough money to build my own home	1
[Renting from RHBMS	12]

Receiving a legacy was a major factor for a third (32%) of respondents – and for a quarter (25%s) the help of a spouse was significant too. It is perhaps of note that almost all the people who had help from their spouses had also received a legacy.

Just over a fifth (21%) had a house before they became a minister. Almost 6% were helped by their church to buy a property

Of the 8% who were able to buy into the property market without help, half were single at the time; one of them , for instance, one was able to buy a house in the South Wales valleys when property was very cheap. One respondent had enough money to build his own home!

One respondent had a house before entering ministry, but like many had to sell it in order to finance his ministerial training.

It is important to note that almost a quarter (23%) ended up renting from the RBMHS. This proportion is not dissimilar to the national figure of 25% or so (250 out of around 1000 retired ministers) renting property from the RMBHS.

On retirement did you move away from your former community?

87% of respondents moved away from their former community. The Church of England insists that on retirement all priests move to another parish "an appropriate distance away", and bishops to a new diocese. The Baptist Union also recommends that a minister move away from the area in which they lived immediately prior to retirement. However, it recognises that moving is not always possible or welcome, and that, for instance, family responsibilities may mean that the minister needs to stay on.

Some respondents felt strongly that moving away is only the right thing to do. "I think it is important to make a new start. It seems unfair to any new minister to stay in the area – church members may still want to relate to the retired minister". Another wrote: "I felt moving away was absolutely right to enable the church to move forward without any influence from me. I had suffered in ministry from a retired minister constantly interfering with what I was doing and I determined *never* to do that to someone else!"

Of the 13% who stayed in the same area in which they had ministered, around 8% are now worshipping in other churches, but some 4% remain members of the churches of which they were the minister. In the words of one: "I have been blessed with two successive ministers at the church who do not see me as a threat, but as a retired colleague who they can call on when necessary. If this had been different, remaining where I ministered for thirty years would have been difficult. I also know that I, like several of my retired colleagues, would probably find it very hard to find a different church which offered worship and service in ways which would feed my soul." Another has become a deacon and is the church treasurer – but is carefully to observe protocols laid down by the Baptist Union.[28]

---

[28] See Paul Goodliff, 'Approaching Retirement', *Ministry Today* 57 (Spring 2012) lists the following protocols:

1. A strictly adhered to 'sabbatical' break from the congregation upon retirement, preferably of at least six months. This helps the 'leaving and cleaving' work of transfer of trust from one pastor to the next. The retired minister should worship elsewhere. It might be possible in certain locations for the minister to remain in the same home, or district, but commit their membership to another Baptist church. Staying put in a locality does not always mean remaining in the same church.

2. No pastoral work in the church should be attempted by the retired pastor without the express permission of its new minister. With time, and confidence in the relationship between the new minister and the previous one (who is now a church member and the pastoral responsibility of their successor), opportunities to serve collaboratively might be offered and indeed welcomed. But the responsibility for this congregation has passed from the retired minister to their successor, and unwanted 'interference' from the former will prove at best unhelpful, and at worst toxic.

3. Permission to officiate at funerals or weddings should only be sought after careful consideration and negotiation. It may be that a church member has expressed in their will that the retired minister should take their funeral service, but this must be negotiated with the new minister, nonetheless. Similarly, when a minister has been in post for many years, and then retires from a church, whether they remain in membership or not, those who were young people earlier in that minister's pastorate might understandably prefer the retired minister to officiate at their wedding, but this should be resisted by the retired minister unless their successor approaches them with particular pastoral reasons why they wish them to undertake that duty.

4. The same principle must apply to church meeting, where this is the governmental instrument. Silence is always preferable to a contribution from the previous minister, and where a contribution is offered, it should be only ever in support of their successor. Concerns that the retired minister might have (and there are legitimate circumstances where this might be so) should not be voiced in public, and only discussed with great discretion and restraint with, say, the Regional Minister.

5. Permission to remain in membership must be explicitly sought by the managing trustees of the church and granted by church meeting. Generally a minister's membership is attached to their holding pastoral office, and ceases when that office is no longer held.

Reflections on the pluses and minuses of moving away

The pluses of staying were for the most part seen in terms of retaining "the support of neighbours and friends". The minuses of leaving were correspondingly leaving good friends: "we missed the many good friendships in the church and in the community when we moved away in retirement"; "It has taken time to fit in and appreciate the new community and surroundings. On the other hand, a plus of moving away is the opportunity "to make a new beginning – and to make new friendships".

Another plus of moving away is "not always bumping into people from the past or the former church". As one put it: "Having had a long pastorate (twenty-one years), it was good that I could not be involved in the ongoing life of the church, hearing people's moans about how things had changed and being asked for my opinion. At the same time, I had a very good relationship with my successor, who had no hesitation about turning to me for advice from time to time and inviting me back for funerals, special anniversaries etc. It was also helpful that the area I moved to was one where I already had friends."

Yet another plus is being able to "explore new areas".

5.   FINANCIAL ISSUES

Just over 80% are in the Baptist Ministers' Pension Fund; 17% respondents are in other pension schemes; the only NSM just draws a state pension.

My/our annual income:

The income 'bands' were too broad: initially I had proposed bands rising in stages of £5,000, but was told that many ministers would find that intrusive. However, less than 8% preferred not to answer this question – "too personal", said one.

As far as those who did respond, the combined income of almost three-quarters (74%) was less than £30K, with just over 28%

receiving less that £20K. A further 17% have a combined income of over £40K: of these around 13% received under £40K; almost 4% received under £50K; and just one respondent received more than £50K.

The 2018 Baptist Union 'standard' stipend is £22,000. The current 2018/2019 full state pension is £8,546 a year. The full 'normal' pension is 50% of the standard stipend, which in 2018 is £22,000: therefore around £11k. This amounts to just over £19,500. According to a former Baptist Union staff member: "This is not so far short of standard stipend, and given the opportunity in early retirement for some small amounts of additional earnings, the income level is not so different to that earned in ministry". However, as we have seen, relatively few retired ministers have taken up paid employment in early retirement. Furthermore, ministers in pastorate receive either rent-free accommodation (according to the Baptist Union this is worth £6,000) or a rent allowance: by contrast retired ministers need to pay for the upkeep of their home or pay rent. In the light of this, ministers retiring experience a substantial drop in income – and all the more so for those whose pension contributions were less than the norm.

However, it is interesting to compare £19,500 which many retired Baptist ministers receive with the recent findings of the *This is Money* financial website (12 Jan 2018): people retiring in 2018 expect an annual income of £19,900 – which is just £400 more than the Baptist 'standard' stipend.

It is important to note that the figures in the survey reflect 'combined' pension income for married retired ministers. By contrast with the spouses of a good number of many younger serving Baptist ministers, most of the ministers' spouses in the survey did not pursue a career of their own – instead the wives (and the spouses in this survey were almost exclusively wives) supported their husbands by adopting the traditional role of a minister's wife, who tended to be an 'unpaid curate' to all intents and purposes.

The Daily Telegraph reported that industry estimates for a comfortable retirement commonly range between £23,000 and

£27,000.[29] That same report included research by the consumer group *Which?*: this found that retired couples need £18,000 a year on average to cover household essentials such as food, utilities, transport and housing needs; this amount rose to £26,000 when allowing for extras such as European holidays and leisure activities.

How well do you feel you are you managing financially?

Nobody said they were "struggling".

10% said they were "just about managing" – this number includes a younger retired minister who has yet to draw his Baptist pension and is currently living on savings.

Almost 18% said they had "enough to live on".

Just over a third (36%) said they were "comfortable" - these included 10% receiving a combined income of less than £20K. Of the almost a quarter (23%) who said that they had "no money problems", one respondent was receiving less than £20K.

The vast majority ministers in this survey appear to be content. Their contentment probably reflects the spirit of Paul's advice to the young Timothy: "There is great gain in godliness combined with contentment... if we have food and clothing, we will be content with these" (1 Tim 6.6-8).

6.   HEALTH ISSUES

How good is your health? [your spouse's health]

Some 13% had "major health concerns" or were not "in the best of health". Around a tenth ((%) were "OK". Over half (64%) claimed to be "fairly healthy" or "in the best of my health for my age".

---

[29] 'How much do I need to retire?', *Daily Telegraph* 3 January 2018.

Significantly, as the detailed raw data reveals, the spouses appeared to be a good deal less fit than the retired ministers!

What forms of regular exercise do you take?

Walking is the favourite form of exercise: around one third (36%) take long walks (some 8% with a dog); and a further third (34%) take either 'moderate walks' or 'occasional long walks' or 'short walks.

Over one fifth (21%) say gardening is one of their forms of exercise; with almost 8% going to a gym.

Other forms of exercise include swimming, cycling, golf, bowls, building, church cleaning, church maintenance, table tennis – for one respondent 'skiing'!

Bearing in mind that many respondents mentioned more than one form of exercise, the impression is that most retired ministers do not exercise much. Almost 6%, however, mentioned that they used to take exercise, but can do so no longer; and on respondent said he only went for short walks, but up until the age of 86 had gone to the gym and had also swum regularly!

7.   LOOKING TO THE FUTURE

The first three questions in this section related to setting our affairs in order.

Have you made a will?

Not surprisingly, with ministers often having to deal with the dying and the bereaved, almost 90% of the respondents had made a will. By contrast, in 2016 only 36% of over 55s in the UK had not made a will.

Have you given somebody a power of attorney (for health and/or for finance)?

Three quarters of retired ministers have not given a power of attorney (for health and/of for finance) to anyone. This power of attorney ensures that one's wishes are observed when one is no longer able to care for oneself.

Have you chosen hymns or readings for your funeral?

Over a third (38%) of retired ministers had chosen hymns or readings for their funeral. No doubt this reflects their own experience how much easier it is to conduct a personal funeral when the wishes of the deceased are known. One respondent commented: "every time I try, new songs emerge that I prefer"!

Do you have any worries about the future?

This question elicited some very different responses: half said no, while half said yes.

On reflection 'worries' may have been the wrong word – 'concerns' might have been better. As one wrote: "I have concerns, but I am not crippled by worry". Another said: "As a Christian I have 'no worries'(was he thinking of Matt 6.25-34 where in the Sermon on the Mount where Jesus told his disciples not to worry?); but there are things I wonder about: my wife is six years older, and so will she die before me? If I die first, will she have enough income?" Several mentioned "keeping independent and keeping my mental faculties". Similarly, for some "the prospect of health limitations with age do not bring great joy, and at some time the prospect of downsizing to a more manageable property isn't attractive". Other concerns included the health of family members; children who were struggling financial, and the wellbeing of a son with Asperger's; and "ultimately having to downsize again" – while another mention his understandable concern for "planet earth"!

8.   RELATIONSHIP WITH GOD

How regular are your daily devotions?

Over 96% were regular in their daily devotions – 68% did so "every day", and 28% "most days" a daily discipline. Of the 4% who are "infrequent" in their daily devotions, one said: "I am constantly aware of God's presence"

What scheme are you currently using for your personal reading of the Bible?

40% use printed Bible reading notes – if online Bible reading notes are included, the percentage rises to 47%. Another 43% read through a Bible book either with or without a commentary. Just over 15% follow the Lectionary of Celtic Daily Prayer. Less than 6% don't have any regular pattern.

It is interesting to contrast the responses of retired ministers with the responses of ministers yet to retire. In a survey of ministers reading habits, the following percentages were obtained: [30]

The Lectionary	13%
Printed Bible reading notes	19%
Online Bible notes/devotional thoughts	19%
Reading through a Bible book with a commentary	19%
Reading through a Bible book without a commentary or notes	36%
I don't have a regular pattern of reading	19%

[The figures would suggest that a few ministers are using more than one scheme]

---

[30] See Paul Beasley-Murray, 'Ministers' Reading Habits', *Baptist Quarterly* 49 [1] (January 2018).

Are you accountable to anyone spiritually?

Three-quarters were not accountable to any one spiritually. Of those who were accountable, nobody had a 'spiritual director'. Instead mention was made of "the pastor: "a prayer triplet" or "a prayer partner"; "a ministers' monthly gathering"; or "informally".

Is there anyone who serves as a mentor to you?

Almost 80% had no mentor. Of those who had, it was not clear how many had a formal arrangement with a mentor. Responses included: retired ministers; old friends; and "unofficially"). Less than 4% who said they had a mentor replied in the earlier question that they were accountable to someone spiritually.

If no [to the two previous questions], would you see any benefit at this stage in having another person have input into your life?

Of the 20% who said they would appreciate a mentor, one answered "Yes, most definitely"; while another said "We always need input". On the other hand, one minister felt that having a person to have input into his life would be "too personal".

I suspect that the quarter (around 26%) who did not answer probably don't see any benefit in having another person to have input in their lives. If so, then this means that over two-thirds (over 70%) see no need for a 'mentor' or somebody to 'accompany' them on their spiritual journey.

Have you been able to continue some biblical and theological study?

Over half (57%) of the respondents in the survey said they had continued to study.

Do you belong to a theological society or study group where you can grow and develop in your theological thinking?

87% did not belong to a theological society or study group. Of those who do, mention was made of "a study group with two other Baptist members"; the "Baptist Historical Society"; "*Societas Liturgica* & the Alcuin club"; "the Cathedral theological society", and the "Society for New Testament Studies".

Commentaries apart, what (if any) theological books have you read in the last three months

Apart from the 5% who said the books they had read were "too numerous to list", the 70% of all respondents who listed the books they had read, averaged three theological books in three months. This is impressive, and not least because a good number of the books they mentioned were relatively demanding.

By contrast around a quarter of retired ministers had done no theological reading in that period. One said: "Now I am not preaching so much, it is more important to know Jesus and God, then just to know about them".

What, if any, non-theological books have you read in the last three months?

Just over half (51%) listed books they had read and these averaged again three non-theological books in a wide variety of fields. The one fifth who had read "too many to list", included "mostly thrillers", "crime novels", "biographies", "mostly epic fantasy novels", and "novels, poetry and history". Another fifth specifically said they had not read anything. Bearing in mind that less than 6% of respondents were women, and that in Britain older women tend to be the avid readers, this again was impressive.

9.   RELATIONSHIP WITH A LOCAL CHURCH

In this survey all respondents are engaged in the worship life of a local church. However, one is still in his first year of retirement and has yet to 'join' a church – this needs to be borne in mind when looking at the responses to the next questions.

Most respondents are still members of a Baptist church: however, just over a quarter (26%) worship in a non-Baptist church – most attend Anglican churches, but some attend another Free or independent church. Reasons for not attending a Baptist church vary: for one, the Baptist church in town is elderly and small; for another the local Baptist church lacks a strong evangelical teaching ministry; others are attracted by the breadth and depth of a more liturgical tradition.

How happy are you in your present church?

Just over half (53%) were either "very happy" (34%) or just "happy" (19%). By contrast under half were either just 'OK' (10%), 'unhappy' (15%), 'very unhappy' (4%). Others were 'unsettled' or had yet to belong to a church.

How supportive is the church to you?

Here the figures are an improvement on the previous question. Almost one third (31%) feel the church is "very supportive"; and another quarter (26%) feel the church is "supportive". One respondent commented: "critically, this is related to us being supportive".

On the other hand, around 40% appear to feel no support. Almost one fifth (19%) feel "treated like any other person"; over one tenth (11.3%) feel "ignored"; and almost one tenth feel "treated with suspicion".

The question arises, in what sense can and should a church be 'supportive' of a retired minister? In what sense did those responding to the questionnaire understand the term 'support'? Is it just the normal kind of 'pastoral' support which any member could expect – or is it more? If, as we shall see, almost every respondent believes that 'ordination is for life', then one might think that churches would continue to honour those retired ministers in their midst as a gift from God to their church (see Eph 4.11).

The survey later reveals that many churches are glad to continue to use the experience of retired ministers by asking them to preach or to share in the church's pastoral care – although this is not the case in every church. Even as the limitations of age increase, there are still surely times when a church can affirm their delight in the presence of these 'honorary' elders amongst them.

How good is your relationship with the minister of your present church?

Almost one third (32%) felt they had a "very good relationship" and another quarter felt they had a "good" relationship. However, although these 57% stated they have a "good" or "very good" relationship with their minister, when later asked "would you count the minister as a friend", only 43% said "yes".

Almost a third (30%) were less positive: 13% said their relationship was "OK", another 11% said their relationship was "not good" and 6% said it was "not good at all"

Some 11% said their church had no minister.

On reflection it might have been interesting to get respondents to reflect on the nature of their relationship with the minister. To what extent is the relationship mutually beneficial? Is the relationship more than pleasantries at the church door? Or is there a deeper sharing of heart and mind? Does the minister take the opportunity to visit his retired colleague on a regular basis – and in the context of growing friendship talk through some of the issues on his heart?

How much do you feel part of your present church?

Here there is a slight increase in those feeling positive towards their church: just under two thirds of respondents feel "very much" (35%) or "quite" (28%) part of the church.

However, over one tenth (11%) feel just "OK"; while a further fifth feel either "on the edge" (13%) or "very much on the edge" (6%) of their present church. This sense of being on the edge must be tough – and all the more so in a Baptist church where traditionally membership is understood as a covenant relationship, in which we are committed "to love one another and stand by one another whatever the cost".[31]

Do you belong to a home group or similar small group?

Most respondents (64%) are involved in their local church during the week through belonging to a home group, of which many are the leader.

I now wish I had asked to what extent the home group really satisfies. I wonder to what extent ministers – even in their retirement – can be just another member of the group, for by virtue of their call to teach and preach, ministers have been called in the first place to be men and women of theology. [32] Retired ministers have spent a life-time dedicated to the study of theology, and that study together with a life-time dedicated to the service of others through the ministry of prayer sets them apart. We cannot pretend others. Yet other members of the church fail to see this. As one commented: "There is little understanding of the peculiarity of my position as a retired minister". Belonging to a home group may help retired ministers to develop friendships (according to one respondent it was the "best part of church") and so contribute to their sense of belonging in the church – but to what extent they meet the

---

[31] A form of words which I always used in welcoming people into church membership

[32] Michael Ramsey, *The Christian Priest Today* (SPCK, London revised ed. 1985) 7.

spiritual needs of retired ministers, let alone contribute to their spiritual development, may be questionable.

Do you belong to other groups in the church?

40% said they did not belong to any other group in the church.

However, 15% were involved with a men's group of some kind; and almost 8% were in positions of leadership such as being a deacon or an elder or a member of the PCC. Other groups included a prayer chain/prayer group; a Bible study group; the choir or music group; groups for preaching, planning worship, running Alpha, exercising pastoral, and church publicity; a lunch club or tea meeting for older people; an art & craft group; a CAP job club; Messy church; Open Book (schools work); a technical team and a maintenance team.

10.   FRIENDS – IN THE CHURCH AND BEYOND THE CHURCH

At two points in the questionnaire I asked about friends: the first-time about friends in the church, and the second time about friends in the wider community.

Have you made friends with the members of the church?

91% had made some friends, but only 36% had "many" friends. 8% had made no friends.

Have you made new friends outside the church?

Although 72% said they had made friends outside the church, only 23% had made "many" new friends outside of the church compared to the 36% who said they had made many new friends in the church. Almost 4% had made some acquaintances, but almost one tenth (9%) had made no friends. What about the fifth (21%) who did not reply? Are they to be included amongst those who had no friends?

On reflection, I should have defined more clearly what I meant by the word 'friend', for I wonder whether the situation is worse than it might appear. For the word friend can cover four different categories of friends:

> Casual friends - friends – acquaintances – people whose names you know

> General friends – people you might invite to your home for a party

> Good friends – people with whom you can begin to be open

> Close friends – our best friends - people with whom you can be completely 'real'.[33]

I suspect that retired ministers have on the whole relatively few "good" or "close" friends.

This variety of meaning became clear when I talked to one retired minister who said he had "many friends" in the church, but in all his time in that church he had never had a meal in anybody's home – nor had he had anybody back home for a coffee.

In the past six months how many church people have invited you into their home?

On reflection I should have asked "how many times have you been invited out by church people either into their home or to a restaurant?" Most answering this question specifically mentioned the number of couples – I have therefore counted a couple as 'one' invitation.

The invitations to a home or out to a restaurant were not overwhelming: less than a third (28%) had been invited out over three times in a six-month period; less than a third (30%) been

---

[33] See Paul Beasley-Murray, 'Levels of friendship', *Church Matters.* See also Kaya Burgess, 'A stranger can become your friend in 90 hours', *The Times* 14 April 2018.

invited out once or twice; and just under a third (32%) had never been invited. If one includes the no responses with those who had not been invited out, then the figure rises to 38%.

One respondent commented, "hospitality does not seem to be part of today's culture"; another wrote: "hospitality is not part of this fellowship". However, 'it takes two to tango'. In the words of another: "This is about being pro-active. We invite people regularly. They invite us." I wonder how much effort some retired ministers have put into making new friends in a new church.

I now wish I had also asked "how many people outside the church have invited you into their home?" I fear that the numbers would have been even lower.

It has been pointed out to me that I did not ask how many retired ministers had invited people into their home – but this deliberate. In so far as it tends to be part of the job for pastors to exercise 'hospitality', I was more interested to see how much friendship was being offered by those who were not retired ministers.

Are there any factors which make it difficult to make friends in the church?

Two-thirds (66%) felt there were no factors involved.

However, one third (34%) felt there were factors. A number mentioned such as 'distance from the church'; 'frequent Sunday absences preaching elsewhere'; 'we are often away'; and even 'middle-class reserve – friendly but distant'. Others said: "I am perceived as 'clever' and 'other' - my interests don't coincide with some of the things that happen at church: e.g. knit and natter group, musical theatre, endless baking"; "my introvert temperament"; "I refuse to be part of a clique"; "I am mindful of the apparent 'hurdle' of being a retired minister"; "I do not try to form the kind of close relationships with members which was appropriate for a pastor"; and even "I prefer not to make friends with church people". One respondent mentioned that many older people find it more difficult to make and maintain friendship in later life than when they were young. [34]

11.   MINISTRY IN RETIREMENT

In this section there were four statements for respondents to 'tick'. I had seen the first two statements standing over against each other, and similarly the last two statements standing over against each other – but this was not made clear in the questionnaire itself.

'God continues to have a call' versus 'the time to withdraw'

Ordination is for life, so God continues to have a call on my life:
                81%

Retirement is the time to withdraw from the demands of ministry   25%

It was significant that 81% claimed that "ordination is for life, so God continues to have a call on my life", for among Baptist churches there has been a debate about the relationship of ministry to the local church. Arthur Dakin, a former principal of Bristol Baptist College, argued that the moment a minister ceases to be the pastor of a Baptist church, that moment he ceases to be a minister – "there is actually no minister without ministering". [35] Indeed, the *Baptist Ministers' Journal* contains a liturgy releasing a retiring minister from ministry. [36]

---

[34] See, for instance, *Age UK Loneliness Review* (revised July 2015) who cite S. Pettigrew, R. Donovan, D, Boldy, & R. Newton, 'Older people's perceived causes of and strategies for dealing with social isolation', *Aging & mental health* 18.7 (2014), 914-920.

[35] See Arthur Dakin, *The Baptist View of the Church and Ministry* (Baptist Union Publications, London 1944).

[36] See 'An Act of Thanksgiving for and Release from Ministry' *BMJ* 280 (October 2002) 11-12 where the congregation says: "We represent the Church of Jesus Christ which called you and set you apart for Ministry. In his name

However, in recent years Baptists have adopted an increasingly 'sacramental' as distinct from a 'functional' approach to ministry, [37] in which ordination is viewed effectively as an 'indelible' act from which there can be no turning back: once a minister, then a minister for ever. [38] This certainly is the understanding of almost all the respondents. Overwhelmingly retired ministers believe that retirement is not the end of ministry.

Less than 6% specifically said ordination is not for life: one, who was trained at Bristol Baptist College, specifically referred to the views of Arthur Dakin; others preferred to speak of God's call to 'Christian discipleship' as being 'for life'.

The second statement was perhaps not best phrased. The word "demands" was clearly understood in more than one way. I had seen this statement as the opposite of the first – whereas in fact seven of those who had agreed with the first statement agreed with the second statement, as if the term "demands" was equivalent to perhaps the term "pressures".

Content to be an ordinary 'punter' versus 'I find it difficult'

On Sundays I am content to be an ordinary 'punter' in the pew
42%

I find it difficult listening to somebody else preach
22%

---

we now release you from your responsibility as Minister and pray God's blessing on the new chapter in your life which is just beginning".

[37] See Paul Goodliff, *Ministry, Sacrament and Representation: Ministry and Ordination in Contemporary Baptist Theology, and the Rise of Sacramentalism* (Regent's Park College, Oxford 2010).

[38] See Paul Beasley-Murray, 'The Ministry of All and the Leadership of Some' 166-167 in *Anyone for Ordination?* (Marc, Tunbridge Wells 1993) ed. Paul Beasley-Murray, where I argue that there is no New Testament warrant for this position!

Within Baptist churches traditionally the call to ministry is seen as primarily a call to preach. Hence 'preaching with a view (to the pastorate)' is at the heart of the process of a local church calling a minister. In the questionnaire I was seeking to discover how retired Baptist ministers cope with that stage in life when they are longer fulfilling what was at the heart of their calling.

The answer is that for over two-fifths, they listen to others preach 'with difficulty'. True, for some it is the quality of the preaching that makes it "difficult listening to somebody else preach", particularly, said one, when it is "without their having been trained and sometimes without much preparation"; but for others, it is simply difficult sitting "in the pew".[39]

Opportunities for the retired to serve God in his church

Many of the retired are busily involved in serving God in his church.

I continue to preach and lead Bible studies:	85%
I look for opportunities to share my faith:	60%
I continue to take funerals:	55%
I help with pastoral care:	47%
I lead a home/small group:	36%
I mentor younger ministers:	21%
I serve as a spiritual director:	2%

Less than 6% are involved as serving as a deacon or an elder. Less than 4% are involved in leading Alpha. Less than 2% are involved in mentoring older ministers or mentoring young leaders in the church; or serving as a volunteer in church café; belonging to a school's worker's support group or taking school

---

[39] One respondent, perhaps rightly, did not approve of my term 'punter'. "I am not a punter", he wrote, "I am there as a worshipping and praying member listening and watching for what God is doing".

assemblies; or running a church bookstall or working in a church library; editing a church newsletter or preacher training or playing the piano and keyboard or serving as a trustee of two charities; or being a church treasurer or church cleaner or chairing the local Churches Together.

It was surprising to see that not every retired minister looks for 'opportunities to share my faith'. Faith-sharing – or evangelism – is part of the Baptist DNA. As the Baptist Union's Declaration of Principle puts it: "It is the duty of every disciple to bear witness to the Gospel of Jesus Christ, and to take part on the evangelisation of the world". Or in the words of Johann Gerhardt Oncken, the great German church planter: "Every Baptist a missionary". Yet for 40% of respondents this appears not to be the case. One who did look to share his faith, said he "seldom" had an opportunity.

12.   RELATIONSHIPS WITH OTHER MINISTERS SINCE RETIREMENT

Do you attend as local ministers meeting?

Less than 10% of retired ministers attend a local ministers meeting. On the whole retired ministers are not welcome at meetings designed for 'active' ministers – and understandably so, for the concerns of the former are different from the concerns of the latter.

Do you belong to a retired ministers' group?

62% belong to a retired ministers groups – but 38% do not. A number indicated there wasn't a group for retired ministers in their area. Where there are groups, my understanding is that all these groups have been set up at the initiative of retired ministers.

38% of respondents indicated they meet up (occasionally) with minister-friends in other parts of the country.

13. RELATIONSHIPS WITH THE BAPTIST UNION AND REGIONAL MINISTERS IN RETIREMENT

Have you had a pastoral visit or personal letter or phone call from your regional minister?

Almost four fifths (79%) had experienced no contact with a regional minister since retirement. Clearly some associations have different policies from others. In the South Eastern Baptist Association, I am told, every retired minister receives a Christmas visit from a regional minister bearing the annual gift of a Christmas cake. The South-Western Association has appointed pastoral care co-ordinators for retired ministers, and these co-ordinators are accountable to one of the regional ministers. But such care is not the norm elsewhere.

This lack of contact is evident, for instance, in the Eastern Baptist Association where 80% had not received a pastoral visit or personal letter or a phone call from their regional minister. Significantly, there were particular reasons for the five respondents within the EBA for receiving a visit, letter, or phone call: one was a member of the same church as one of the regional ministers; one is a personal friend of one of the regional ministers; one had himself been a regional minister and so could be regarded as having been a colleague; one asked for a visit, and the fifth was visited by a regional minister with a view to him becoming moderator of a church. Of those EBA ministers who had not had any contact with a regional minister, one stated: "I wrote to him twice, but received no acknowledgement or reply". Another said: "Even after the death of my wife I had no contact".

How often do you have opportunities to preach in churches in your Association?

Although in a previous question 85% of respondents were involved in "preaching and leading Bible studies", the resulting figures are considerably lower when it comes to preaching invitations in the local church:

Almost half appear to want to preach, but either have never preached (17%) or have preached once (2%) or have preached only "rarely" or "occasionally" (30%).

Over a quarter appear to preach "regularly": these include those who each once or twice as month (13%); who preach only in their local church (4%), or who preach "very often" (2%).

A quarter do not seek preaching invitations on grounds of personal ill-health or the ill-health of a spouse or simply because they no longer wish to preach.

I sense a degree of frustration on the part of some that they do not preach more often.

Other involvement in association life

32% have been to an association assembly

28% have served as a moderator of another church

25% have been to an association ministers' conference

17% have been asked to do a task in another church

Most retired ministers have clearly no longer any involvement in the association. This involvement is even more limited than it might appear, since for many attendance at an assembly or a ministers' conference has been a one-off. Some respondents have mentioned the cost – especially of the minister's conference.

Involvement in wider Baptist life

36% read the electronic *Baptist Times*

32% have been to the Baptist Assembly

Here too we see limited involvement – even when it comes to reading regularly the *Baptist Times*. A number of respondents said they would read the *Baptist Times* if it appeared as a hard copy.

How much do you feel part of the Baptist family?

Two-fifths (43%) still feel "part of the wider Baptist family – and a further 3% feel "very much". But most do not feel they belong any more. Even one respondent who said that he still "feels part of the wider Baptist family", feels "marginalised".

Almost three-tenths (28%) "feel neither one thing or another". This includes one respondent who commented "my only link is the pension scheme".

Just over one fifth say they "no longer feel part of the wider Baptist family"; and 15% say they "feel forgotten by the wider Baptist family".[40]

These are sobering statistics, and all the more so in that here we are not dealing with ordinary church members, but with ministers who have given a life-time of service to the Baptist family. Whereas in this post-modern age many members of Baptist churches today are only members because they 'feel' good to be members of a particular Baptist church – and if they were to move away to another town are just as likely to join a church of another denomination where the worship or the preaching or the love of the fellowship may 'feel' good – here we are dealing with men and women who are Baptists by conviction. Itis significant that earlier in the questionnaire, when respondents were asked "would they want to belong to a different denomination", the overwhelming consensus was "yes" – if God were to call them into ministry again, the only option would be Baptist ministry. Only one respondent answered "possibly". This is the context in which we need to consider the responses to the question: "How much do you feel part of the wider 'Baptist family'". It is surely food for thought that so many feel they have been let down by the wider Baptist family.

---

[40] Some of these figures may appear not to add up, but this is because some respondents ticked more than one response: e.g. "I no longer feel part of the wider Baptist family" and "I feel forgotten by the wider Baptist family".

Are you content with the support you currently receive?

75% are not content with the support they receive. This is a devastating response. Indeed, one response was "What support?". Within the context of 'relationships with the Baptist Union and regional ministry, this is surely a cause for great disease.

It is important to realise that the context of this question is on the relationship with the Baptist Union and its regional ministers. In addition to the 25% who are content, a further 15% say that they are content with the support they receive, but explicitly state that it is not "thanks to Baptists", or at least "not thanks to the Baptist Union and its regional ministers".

One, who did not receive support from the association or Union, said: "I don't expect support from the Baptist family staff. You have to get on with it and find people to journey with". However, he and his wife are in the unusual position of being in a church where there are two other retired ministers and their wives, with whom they meet up on a regular basis.

Other comments include: "The silence was deafening and continues"; "I would like regional ministers to know that I exist"; "There was virtually no support from the Area Ministry team: it was left to the initiative of a locally well-known retired minister to bring other retired ministers and spouses together. I'm not complaining but it's almost as though we became 'invisible' to the BU and the Area"; "It would be nice to have had regular follow-up from the regional team to make sure retirement was working".

If you are not content with the support you receive, then how do you feel churches, associations and indeed the Baptist Union could better support retired ministers?

At this point many comments were made. Regional ministers need "to recognise that we have a vast library of gathered ministerial knowledge that is left untapped for the most part". "There needs to be some acknowledgement we exist – as it is there is no Baptist Union handbook (in which are names used to appear); and the names of retired ministers no longer appear in association handbooks". "It is a great shame that the Association makes no provision for retired ministers to meet from time to time. We do get a printed card from the team at Christmas, but that does not add up to pastoral care". "The Baptist Steering Group [of the Baptist Union] seems to assume that pastoral care of ministers was solely the responsibility of the local church (questions asked via the Baptist Ministers Fellowship & the Retired Baptist Ministers Housing Association): in other words, retired ministers are no different from other retired people". One of the saddest comments was, "I feel so far removed that I cannot offer any suggestions".

Along with others one respondent urged: "Make the visitation of retired ministers a high priority for area ministers, who seem to forget we exist but who would benefit from our wisdom and experience". Another wrote: "I know regional ministers' time is pressured and resources are limited, but I think one regional minister in each association should have responsibility for the retired minister in their area and keep in regular contact by phone or e-mail or by arranging meetings. A phone call once in a while to ask 'How you're doing' would be nice! By definition, pastoral care should be offered, not sought in an emergency". Yet another said: "I feel ministers enter ministry 'with a bang' (e.g. recognition at Assembly) and leave with a whimper. The Baptist Union is 'missing a trick' in not using the example of 'life-long' ministry as an inspiration to those coming into and possibly struggling in ministry. It's more about recognition than support really. There is also a reluctance on the part of some regional leaders to see the value that retired ministers could bring to ministers' meetings provided they did not harp back to 'how it was done in my day' but encourage other ministers in their struggles which most of us have been through." A similar comment was expressed by another respondent: "For a number of years, I was a member of the Association Board of Trustees. One of my often-repeated suggestions was to draw attention to the number of "young" (newly retired) ministers living in the Association with a wealth of skills and experience that the Association might use to their advantage".

14. RELATIONSHIP WITH THE FAMILY

Some fourteen questions were asked about family relationships, but many of them proved not to be of great significance. For instance, as might be expected most retired ministers do not have elderly parents to care for – indeed, only six did. As one respondent said: "We are elderly parents/grandparents"!

'How has retirement affected your spouse?'

Some spouses clearly found the transition difficult. For instance: "It has been difficult fitting into church life – change of roles"; "she misses people very much and can feel lonely"; "it has not been easy having to uproot once more and set up new relationships – but she is very resilient"; "she has found it more difficult that I have leaving some very close friends in our last church and feeling quite unhappy here with issues with the house etc. She is more content now and is finding a few roles in the church."

Some spouses appreciated the transition. For instance, "she is pleased to be free from church 'politics'; "she is able to have meaningful friendships more than when I was a minister"; "she now appreciates the possibility of being an "ordinary" member of the church and not having to live up to people's expectations; "Instead of duties she now has choices"; "she is very happy with it".

For two spouses retirement is entailing fresh opportunities: one "has taken on spiritual direction and runs the diocese training course for new spiritual directors"; another is seeking to re-establish opportunities to continue her piano tuition in a new area".

How has retirement affected your relationship with your spouse?

For some "not much has changed"; "our relationship is as strong as before".

For others retirement appears to have enhanced relationships: "we have grown closer together, become more interdependent, but have also lost some individual independence"; "we pray together more, we sit in church together"; "we have more time together – especially evenings"; "we have more time to do things together – we have taken the opportunity to foster involvement in activities outside the church and we also appreciate having weekends to visit family and friends".

Involvement in church life

By comparing the answers on the number of children and grandchildren, and the answers on how many of their children were still involved in church life, and how many of their grandchildren attend church, the following figures emerged:

> 49% of children of the Manse are involved in church life – 51% are not. 53% of grandchildren of retired ministers attend church – and 47% do not.

The church statistician, Peter Brierley, quoted some Canadian research which showed that just over 53% of children follow their parents' faith, with just over 46% no longer attending church – however, these figures apply to children from Christian families in general, not to 'children of the manse' – or rather to children of ministers now retired.[41]

The questionnaire did not ask respondents to give a reason as to why any of their children were no longer involved in church life. However, respondents did mention how time and again the behaviour of people in the church had proved a stumbling block. One wrote, for instance, that his son "turned away from the church, but not from Jesus Christ, because of the mismatch between faith and Christian behaviour toward me in some leading Christians at a key time in his life. I received a letter of apology from that Christian community for this behaviour, but

---

[41] Peter Brierley, *Pulling Out of the Nosedive* (Christian Research, London 2008) 115.

the damage had been done – and it remains to this day in his life". Another wrote: "I regret the extent to which they were probably affected by times of extreme tension". Yet another wrote of the loss of faith of three of his children caused by the way in which they had seen their father "abused" in the contest of a church "fight". [42] Hopefully, perhaps not all is lost. As one retired minister commented: "sadly our three are not involved with church now, but they do have fond memories of some of the things they did as part of church".

15.   RELATIONSHIP WITH THE WIDER WORLD

New Interests

The involvement of retired ministers in 'the wider world' was somewhat limited:

40% work as a volunteer in the community

19% have developed new IT skills

17% go regularly/occasionally to the theatre, cinema, concert hall

9% have done a cookery course

8% have become a Rotarian (or equivalent)

8% attend study courses linked with U3A/Workers Educational Institute/ etc

6% have joined a political party

4% now belong to a book club:

---

[42] See Patricia Fouque, 'Abuse in Ministry', *Ministry Today* 10 (Summer 1997) 10: "Children of the Manse or Vicarage carry heavy burdens, and when there is conflict in the church or their father is dismissed from post, they have to face not only a change of school friends, church, but also their parents' pain. Many are left with a deep sense of betrayal and struggle well into adult years, with feelings of bitterness, resentment and anger."

Other interests mentioned included playing golf (6%); wood-turning (4%); carpet/indoor bowls (4%); and joining a local choir (4%). Less than 2% mentioned starting piano lessons or and developing skills on piano and organ; joining an art group; exploring family history; becoming an Advanced Driving mentor; building a model railway; looking after fish; watching cricket, rugby and football; and after-dinner speaking.

Recognising that some retired ministers are engaged in more than one activity, we can conclude that a large proportion of retired ministers do not seem to be relating to the wider community in which they are set, and therefore they would appear not to be fulfilling their calling to be 'salt' and 'light' in the world (Matt 5.13-16).

16.   EXPERIENCE OF RETIREMENT SO FAR

What is the best thing you enjoy about retirement?

Freedom, together with variations on the theme, was the only and almost exclusive reply of 87% of respondents: "freedom to serve God on my own terms; "freedom and a more relaxed life; "freedom to choose what I do"; "freedom to say 'no'"; "freedom to go and watch Essex County Cricket"; "not having responsibility"; "freedom from pressure"; "flexibility"; "freedom from 'must do' pressure"; "free - not having to go our every evening"; "space to read a novel, to think, to meet regularly with friends and talks"; "free to have time for family and going away a lot"; freedom from time pressure; freedom to do things; freedom to travel.

There were only four other individual responses: "being able to work for love rather than pay"; the opportunity to go on being of service within the church; "living in my home", and "living in a lovely place". [43]

---

[43] By contrast a 2017 Legal and General Survey of 2000 of their pensioners indicated that only 12% of their respondents mentioned 'freedom' as one of

What is the hardest challenge you face in retirement?

Here the responses were more diverse:-

Growing older	15%
Loneliness	11%
Living life meaningfully	11%
Time	9%
Being a carer	8%
Loss of role	8%
Church	8%
Money	2%
No challenges	6%

The following comments were received:

Being a carer: "caring for a very sick wife"; "caring for my wife"; "helping our son who has Asperger's Syndrome find his way through life".

Church: "A dreadful experience of the local Baptist church"; "integration with a church I find difficult"; "disappointment with the church we attend"; "hearing about the churches where I have ministered and the fact that they are declining."

Getting older: "motivation and relative immobility due to disability"; "accepting the need to slow down"; "acceptance of limitation"; "growing old and less able"; "not being able to do all the things I used to and the things I still can do take so much longer"; "declining physical ability"; "coming to terms with changing physical capability"; "decreasing energy"; "health issues"

Leaving life meaningful: "self-indulgence becomes tedious for those whose calling is to live for others in the service of Christ"; "struggling with purpose and knowing who I am"; "boredom"; "to find out who I am now that my wife has died and having to

---

the good aspects of retirement. Other good aspects mentioned with no time pressure (25%), hobbies (12%), grandkids/family (9%) and travelling (6%).

make a new life for myself"; "the reduction in personal fulfilment"; relaxing and not thinking I'm wasting time; "remembering my worth before God is not based on what I achieve in ministry but who I am by his grace"

Loneliness: "times when lonely"; "missing good friends in my pastorates"; "loneliness since my wife died and self-motivation"; "living the life of a bachelor after 57 years of married life"; "long dark nights on my own"; "spending long dark winter evenings at home"

Loss of a role: "having something to offer when it is not apparently accepted"; "not having gifts used"; "remembering my worth before God is not based on what I achieve in ministry but who I am by his grace".

Time: "wanting to fully retire but seeing the challenges in and outside church life for authentic Christian service"; "time to do everything I want to"; "not allowing time to slip by" "the temptation to take on too many commitments"; "getting a balance in time spent between the things we have to do and the things we want to do. "Retirement is a job to be negotiated – we find that we have to book a day off each week since if we do not do this, then it fails to happen, and we can easily find ourselves without much time to actually do relaxing things together".

Money: "We would like a little more money". [44]

What are you still passionate about?

Apart from one respondent who said "I don't do passion", a wide range of passions could be discerned. Amongst the many responses, there were five main themes:

---

[44] By contrast in the 2017 Legal and General Survey of 2000 of their pensioners the following "bad" aspects were mentioned: financial worries (14%), getting older (11%), health worries (9%), missing work social life (8%); nothing – I enjoy everything (65).

The Gospel	47%
The Church	40%
The Kingdom	36%
Life	34%
My family	11%

Passion for the Gospel included passion for evangelism, world mission, Biblical but reasoned witness, relating faith and science, Biblical truth and young people

Passion for the Church included village churches, community, discipleship, prayer preaching, doing things well in the name of Christ, and church history

Passion for the Kingdom includes inclusiveness, justice, older people, peace, the persecuted, politics, the poor and the powerless, and overseas aid.

Passion for life included the arts together with music and painting, birdwatching, food, the French language, gardening, travel and walking, and a sport (golf; Irish rugby; Chelsea, Manchester United and Norwich City football clubs; Surrey & England cricket).

Passion for the family included 'my wife'

General reflections on your experience of retirement

Almost three quarters (74%) are "happy to be retired" – but the inference is that the other quarter (26%) are apparently not happy. One, however, said: "I am getting there".

Just under two thirds (62%) said that "retirement has given me new opportunities to serve God" – but the inference is that the other third (34%) have not taken these new opportunities. By contrast 11% said they were "still searching for purpose".

Only just over half (53%) were "glad to pursue new interests outside the church" – but the inference is that the other half are not pursing any new interests outside the church.

I had assumed that those who are "glad to pursue new interests outside the church" might have also viewed retirement as giving "new opportunities to engage with the wider community": however, of the 42% who ticked the latter statement, only 25% ticked the former statement. Interestingly, of the 42% who said that "retirement has given me opportunities to make friends outside the church", only 13% had ticked both the statement relating to "new interests outside the church" and the statement relating to "new opportunities to engage with the wider community". Cross-checking differently, the number of those seeing retirement giving opportunities both "to engage with the wider community" and "to make friends outside the church" rose to 28%; and the number of those seeing retirement as giving opportunities both to pursue new interests outside the church" and "to make friends outside the church" also rose to 28%.

Under half of the respondents (45%) viewed retirement "an opportunity to relax and rest". The inference is that just over half (55%) therefore did not think of retirement "as the 'Sabbath' of life; the evening's rest awaiting us at the end of a lifetime of work and responsibility". [45] Indeed, 19% said that "in retirement they were busier than ever". In the light of past surveys in which the average working week for many ministers can exceed or sixty hours a week, such a statement is perhaps questionable. [46] On the other hand, maybe the statement is not to be taken literally, but is simply an indication for many life in retirement is 'full'.

I had initially wondered whether the statement "retirement gives new opportunity to play" might be coupled with "an opportunity to relax and rest". However while 42% ticked the former statement and 45% the latter statement, only 17% respondents ticked both statements – as if many do not regard "play" as a form of relaxation!

---

[45] David Winter, *The Highway Code for Retirement* (CWR, Farnham 2012) 22.

[46] See *Power for God's Sake* 47-49: on average ministers reckoned they worked 64.3 hours per week.

42% said retirement had given "opportunities to travel and see more of God's world". On reflection it might have been interesting to ask a question relating to the nature of the travel – one respondent, for instance, spoke of travelling by caravan around the UK.

Just over a third (38%) agreed that "retirement is a great adventure". 4% preferred to speak of retirement as "a new chapter", but this is not the same thing.

For 6% "retirement has proved fairly boring": all 6% together with a further 8% - i.e. 14% in total - had found retirement to be "a lonely experience".

Finally, 13% felt that "retirement has led to a restriction in life". Again, on reflection it might have been helpful to get respondents to indicate the nature of the restriction: clearly for some respondents the restriction related to increasing old age; whereas 4% appear to regard the whole experience of retirement as restrictive, for they also described retirement as "boring".

I am conscious that we are dealing here with relatively small numbers, and that therefore we cannot apply too much weight to percentages. Furthermore, we risk the danger of inferring too much from the silence of those who did not tick one statement or another. Nonetheless, the picture which emerges is that while some ministers are clearly making the most of the opportunities which retirement has to offer, many are not. This surely should be a cause of concern – and for action to be taken to help more retired ministers enjoy the "fulness of life" Jesus came to bring (see John 10.10). Hopefully the guide to retirement in the final section might be of help to some.

SECTION THREE: RETIRED MINISTERS MATTER! A CHALLENGE TO THE BAPTIST UNION OF GREAT BRITAIN AND ITS ASSOCIATIONS

75% OF RETIRED BAPTIST MINISTERS ARE NOT CONTENT

This survey has revealed that there is a strong feeling among many retired Baptist ministers that they have been "abandoned into retirement" by the Baptist Union, and "ignored and neglected" by the associations.

The current stance of the Baptist Union that there is an 'understanding' that the local church is responsible for the care of retired ministers is disingenuous. This is only an understanding between the Baptist Union and its regional ministers: the churches and their ministers are not aware of this understanding – and the experience of many retired ministers is that this delegation of care is not working. In this survey we found

40% feel they have no support from their local church

43% said the minister was not their friend

19% said they felt 'at the edge' or 'very much at the edge' of the church

Some might wonder why the Baptist Union should have a responsibility for its retired ministers. Many teachers, for instance, have a tough time during their working life, but they do not expect any special treatment in their retirement – so why should retired ministers? Other people struggle with their loss of role in retirement – so why should retired ministers expect special care?

Retired ministers are in a special category

They have been – and still are – God's gift to his church. The denomination has a responsibility to help them fulfil that ongoing call which most retired ministers feel God has still upon their lives

99

The denomination has a moral duty to recognise the sacrifices that so many ministers have made. Here I have in mind not the financial sacrifices – although they have been considerable. Rather these men and women have given themselves unstintingly to the service of others – no other profession has as its recommended terms of appointment just one day free a week. In the course of their ministries many have had bad experiences of God's people, and have suffered as a result. Just as the military care for their wounded, so too should we.

Unlike others, when ministers retire they lose not just their role and status, they lose their friends and most lose their homes and in the process often have to lose many of their possessions. Almost all retired ministers have to move and start life afresh in a new community. Retirement is a major challenge for ministers.

A final complicating factor is that although retired ministers stop leading a church, they do not stop attending a church. Unlike most other retired people, they cannot totally withdraw from the work-place – instead they have to watch others doing their former job!

As a denomination we have entered into a life-long covenant to support our ministers. Baptists therefore have an ongoing duty of care for their retired ministers.

SUPPORTING THE MINISTRY OF RETIRED CLERGY: AN ANGLICAN WAY

Supporting the ministry of retired clergy provides advice to Anglican dioceses on how they should care for their retired clergy. [47] In spite of the ecclesiological differences between the Church of England and the Baptist Union of Great Britain,

---

[47] The advice is issued by the Remuneration and Conditions of Service Committee of the Archbishops' Council: first published in June 2007, it was later updated in June 2014.

Baptists have much to learn from this through-provoking guide. Let me quote from this 26-page 'advice'.

Foreword

"Ordination to the Priesthood, in the Church of England, is understood as a life-long vocation... Ordained ministers are called, without any limit of time, as long as they live, to proclaim the glory of God in every part of their lives, not just in the exercise of celebrating public services.... This advice has been produced to assist bishops and archdeacons in supporting retired clergy and enabling them to continue to contribute towards the Church's mission and ministry in a way that is beneficial both for them and for the Church."

Preparation for retirement

"Ten years before the likely date of retirement is not too soon to be actively considering the question of retirement housing.... Discussions about preparation for retirement can usefully be raised as a matter of course during ministerial review from age 60... Clergy should attend a [pre-retirement] course any time after reaching their 55th birthday... Some dioceses have found it useful to have a number of suitably qualified recently retired clergy supported and commended by the bishop, to meet clergy and their spouses... around the age of 55 and between three and one year before retirement."

At retirement

"It is often desirable for the diocesan bishop – or a member of his senior team – to meet clergy, when they retire from ministry. Likewise it may also be helpful, when they move to another diocese on retirement or subsequently, for them to see the bishop of a member of his senior team to discuss the kind of ministry they might be able to offer."

Retirement officers

"Initial pastoral care is the responsibility of the appropriate parish priest. Bishops should appoint retirement officers to assist in meeting these recommendations... Retirement officers may appoint a 'visitor' in each deanery, who will undertake to keep in touch with retired clergy, including visiting them once a year (unless the retired cleric does not want this)... Parish clergy should refer all cases of sickness, bereavement, financial or other needs to a retirement officer or visitor, who should, depending on the level of response needed or pastoral care required, notify the bishop or archdeacon and suggest appropriate help."

The deployment of retired clergy

"Retired clergy are a reservoir of theological, spiritual, counselling and other experience, available to the church.... The purpose of all ministry is to further the Kingdom rather than to affirm the status of the minister.... If a retired cleric finds him/herself at odds with the vision of their incumbent the bishops... should try to find a nearby parish where the retired cleric can minister harmoniously with another incumbent..."

Further ways of supporting the ministry of retired clergy

"Many retired clergy will wish to participate in the annual renewal of ordination vows, and should be encouraged in this.... Bishops are encouraged to offer the opportunity for an annual gather for retired clergy... Other social events may be organised if there is interest....

It may also be desirable to encourage the retirement officers and visitors to ensure that there is celebration and appropriate marking of milestone birthdays and significant anniversaries."

HONOURING THE MINISTRY COVENANT: A BAPTIST WAY

The ministerial covenant

At the heart of Baptist ecclesiology is the concept of covenanting together. John Smyth, for instance, defined a "visible community of saints" as "two or more joined together by covenant with God and themselves... for their mutual edification and for God's glory". There has been an increasing recognition among Baptists of the need to rediscover their roots and realise afresh that, in becoming church members, we enter into a 'covenant' which involves 'covenant relationships'. [48]

In 2001 the Baptist Union produced *Covenant 21 – a Covenant for a Gospel People* with a view to it being used not just within the local church, but also within associations and the Baptist Union itself: "We come this day to covenant with you and with companion disciples to watch over each other and to walk together before you in ways known and to be made known".

In recent years British Baptists have adopted a covenant understanding of the relationship between ministers (including retired ministers) and the Baptist Union: those who are accredited by the Baptist Union "have entered into a covenant with the Baptist Union to live in conformity with the way of life this high calling demands and to receive from the Union such support, recognition and trust as befits those who serve Christ in this way". [49] The *Ignite Report* (December 2015) whose recommendations have been largely accepted by the Baptist Union Council and are in the process of being worked upon, states in its section on 'Living in Covenant Relationship, that "we sense a need to re-state and reclaim our Baptist understanding of covenant ministry", but nowhere speaks of retired ministers as belonging to this ministry covenant.[50] This omission is regrettable – and hopefully in future discussions by the Baptist Union Council consideration will be given to how this ministry covenant can be made more relevant to the needs of retired Baptist ministers.

---

[48] "In a Baptist church, membership involves entering into a dynamic covenant relationship with one another - a relationship in which we commit ourselves not only to work together to extend Christ's Kingdom, but also to love one another and stand by one another whatever the cost". See Paul Beasley-Murray, *Radical Believers: The Baptist way of being the church* (Baptist Union of Great Britain, Didcot 2nd edition 2006) 72 – 76.

[49] Preface to the *Ministerial Recognition Rules relating to the Register of Nationally Accredited Ministers*, adopted by the Council of the Baptist Union of Great Britain on 13 October 2016.

[50] See *Ignite Report* 27-28.

However, as the analysis of the data of this report on retired ministers shows, the current 'ministerial covenant' between the Baptist Union and retired ministers has – with some exceptions – largely broken down. For the most part there is no 'support', no 'recognition', and no 'trust'. [51]

Ministry beyond retirement

If, as almost all the respondents in this survey have stated, God has still a call on the lives of retired ministers, then this needs to be more clearly recognised by the Baptist Union and its associations. Retirement may mark the end of leading a church, but it does not mark the end of ministry. The pace of life may have changed, but most ministers when they retire are still keen to use their experience and energy in the service of God. Of course, the day will come when health and strength will fail, and ministers will need to make the transition from active retirement to a more passive form of retirement – but in the meantime many have a good number of years before they enter into their 'second retirement'. Yet currently most retired ministers receive no help from the Baptist Union and its associations to continue to live out their call – it is left to the retired to take the initiative to discover opportunities for service, and that is not always easy.

Many who entered ministry with a deep sense of God's call find that at retirement they are regarded simply as 'employees' whose time of service to the 'company' or 'firm' is over. This is a secular view of retirement and fails to recognise the ongoing call of God on their lives. When the time comes for ministers to hand over the responsibility of leading a church, the Baptist

---

[51] One exception to this breakdown in the covenant is found in the concern shown by the Head of Ministries in cases where he is told – normally by a regional team minister – of the death of a retired minister. Andy Hughes, the current Head of Ministries, tells me that in such cases he sends a letter of condolence and a gift of £250 from the Baptist Union. However, it is important to note that this only happens when the Head of Ministries is notified of a death: for reasons of data protection the Baptist Pension Trust is not allowed to inform the Baptist Union of a death of a retired minister!

Union and its associations should help ministers to discover what God wants them to do next and where they can best serve him and his church. Not to do so is to deny tried and tested vocations and to deprive churches of a wealth of leadership resource.

Louis Armstrong, the great jazz musician once said: "Musicians don't retire; they stop when there's no more music in them". That too is how many retired ministers feel: they still have divine music in their souls and they will only stop giving voice to that music when they join the greater chorus in heaven! [52]

A way forward

With much of Baptist Union life now delegated from the 'centre' (Didcot) to the 'regions' (associations), regional ministers have a key role to play in ensuring the well-being of retired ministers. Regional ministers are not to be equated with 'bishops' – Baptists have a very different understanding of the nature of the church from Anglican. [53] They do, however, represent the Baptist Union in their associations, and have a key role in implementing the covenant between retired ministers and the Baptist Union.

Precisely how regional ministers might implement the ministry covenant is open for discussion. Although the Baptist Union now has double – if not treble – the number of regional ministers compared with the old 'superintendency' system, there is no doubt that with the delegation of so much Baptist Union life to the regions, they no longer have as much time to care for the ministers in their association as did the previous generations of area superintendents. [54] In my judgment the only

---

[52] I am grateful for this analogy to Canon Hugh Dibbens, who in his retirement serves as the Evangelism Adviser in the Barking Episcopal Area of the Diocese of Chelmsford.

[53] See Paul Beasley-Murray, *Radical Believers* 122-124.

[54] In *Gathering for Worship: Patterns and Prayers for the Community of Disciples* (Canterbury Press, Norwich 2005) ed by Christopher Ellis & Myra

way in which regional ministers can care effectively for retired ministers in their association is to delegate much of the day-to-day care to a small group of 'retirement officers' – perhaps made up of ministers in the first stages of retirement – who would serve as mentors and if not even as pastors to the ministers in their care. From time to time the 'retirement officers' would then report back to their regional ministers. [55]

The appointment of such 'retirement officers' does not remove from churches which have retired ministers in their congregations their duty of care. As with the Anglican system, the local church has a primary duty of care. Ideally churches and retirement officers would work together, with churches taking the initiative in informing retirement officers of any significant pastoral issues.

However, retired ministers need more than pastoral care – they need to be helped to discover how they might continue to respond to God's call. Retirement offices could have a key role to play: not simply in visiting but also in putting in place a programme of mentoring. The first six months of retirement could be regarded as a 'sabbatical' during which ministers could begin to adjust to what for most will be a new home, a new church, and a new community. After six months, however, many will be ready take on new opportunities of service.

My proposal is that, as with the Anglican system, retirement officers would help ministers prepare for retirement through one or more 'exit interviews', and continue to care for ministers in retirement through annual visits. The personal touch – and not emails – is what is wanted. Pastoral care will involve not simply being there for the crises in life – it will also involve

---

Blyth, 11, regional ministers are asked the following people-centred question: "Do you accept the charge from Christ to care for his people with all faithfulness and compassion, watching over the life of the churches with all humility? Will you care for the weak, bring Christ's healing to the broken hearted, lift up the downcast, and pray regularly for those committed to you care?"

[55] It may be that in a Baptist context it would be more helpful to talk of 'association mentors for the retired' rather than 'association retirement officers' – the function rather than the term is ultimately what concerns me.

helping retired ministers to find meaning ways in which they can continue to express the call that God has on their lives.[56]

Retirement officers will help regional ministers organise gatherings – at least once a year – when retired ministers and their spouses are invited to meet with the regional ministers, and ideally with the President of the Baptist Union too (would it be possible to encourage all presidents in their association visits to make time to meet with retired ministers?).

Inevitably there would be a cost to this new system of pastoral care for retired ministers. Although I do not envisage any remuneration for the new 'retirement officers', clearly their travel costs and other expenses would have to be met. Similarly, the costs of an annual social event for retired ministers would need to be paid for. The production and circulation of agreed guidelines for the pastoral care of retirement ministers which would need to go not just to retired ministers but also to all ministers in pastoral charge (otherwise how would they know they have a primary duty of care for retired ministers?) would also entail a cost. However, I would envisage the limited costs would not be a burden on the funds of the Baptist Union and its associations.

The fact is retired ministers need to be honoured – rather than forgotten. They have borne the heat of the day – they have served God faithfully against all the odds. Retired ministers matter!

---

[56] On a different but related note, ministers' widows also need to be cared for, for many of them have also served God faithfully. Perhaps their welfare could be part of the brief of the proposed 'Retirement Officers'?

APPENDIX: THE RAW DATA

1. GENERAL QUESTIONS

Gender
Male:	50
Female	3

Marital status
Never married:	3
Married:	42
Divorced & remarried	1
Widowed	7

Age
Under 65:	2
65-70:	12
70-75:	19
75-80:	9
80-85:	7
85-90:	2
90-95:	1

For a comparison with retired Baptist ministers in the Baptist Pension scheme see the following table provided by Mark Hynes, the Pensions Manager of the Baptist Pension Trust Limited on 4 December 2017:

Status	Under 65	65 – 70	70-75	75-80	80-85	85-90	90-95	95-100	100-105
Pensioner	67	267	230	158	90	46	27	9	2
Dependant	29	13	26	28	35	35	19	7	3
Total	96	280	256	186	125	81	46	16	5

How old were you when you retired?

Under 65	16
65	29
66-70	7
No reply	0

How long have you been retired from stipendiary ministry?

Less than 5 years:	11	
5-10 years:	19	
11-15 years:	8	
16-20 years:	11	+ 1 NSM
21-25 years:	1	
26+ years	1	

2. PAST EXPERIENCE OF MINISTRY

How many years did you serve in stipendiary ministry?

11-15 years:	2	
16-20	7	+ 1 NSM
21-25	3	
26-30	5	
31-35	6	
36-40	19	
41-45	8	

Did you have a good experience of ministry?

It was very tough – my ministry was often rejected:	0
It was tough and often unrewarding	1
There good times, but there were difficult times too	13
For the most part it was rewarding, but there were tough times	38
I have had a wonderful time	1

If you had an opportunity to begin life again, would you want to be a minister?

Yes	30
Only if called	10
Probably not in today's Baptist Union	10
Probably not	3
No	0

Would your spouse want to be married to a Baptist minister?

Yes:	28
Yes, if called	5
Probably not	5
Unsure	5
No	3
Married only for love	3
Unmarried	3
Widowed	3
She would want to be a minister	1
Too personal	1

Would your children want to be involved again in church life?

Yes:	18
Some/one would, the other/s not:	8
Unsure	14
No	5
No children	8

3.   TRANSITION TO RETIREMENT

Did you receive helpful advice?

From a Baptist Union retirement course:	29	+ 2 'only partially'
From other retired people	19	
From books:	7	
From regional ministers	2	

From a financial advisor   1

No   20

What emotions did you feel in the first months of retirement?

Relief	27
Joy	22
Loneliness	8
Depression/deep sadness	6
Frustration	4

Do you still miss being the minister of a church?

Yes	26
A little	2
No	20
Yes and no	5

4.   HOUSING ISSUES

How difficult was the issue of housing for retirement?

Very difficult:	2
Difficult:	4
OK:	17
Easy:	11
Very easy:	19

How did you afford to buy your own home?

I received a legacy from parents/family members	17
My spouse made it possible	13
I had a house before I became a minister:	11
I was helped by my church	3
I had enough money to buy my own house	4
I had enough money to build my own home	1
[Renting from RHBMS	12]

On retirement did you move away from your former community?

Yes: 46

No: 7

5.   FINANCIAL ISSUES

My/our annual income:

Under 20K: 15

Under 30K   24

Under 40K   7

Under 50K   2

Over 50K   1

No answer   4

How well do you feel you are you managing financially?

I am struggling   0

I am just about managing   5

I have enough to live on   17

I am comfortable   19

I have no money problems   12

6.   HEALTH ISSUES

How good is your health? [your spouse's health]

I have major health concerns	2	[7]
I am not in the best of health	5	[5]
I am OK	9	[8]
I am fairly healthy	20	[13]
I am in the best of health (for my age)	14	[5]
No answer	3	

Note that two of the spouses are men, and that three of the retired ministers are women.

What forms of regular exercise do you take?

Long walks	19 (four with dogs!)
Moderate walks	1
Occasional long walks	5
Short walks	12
Occasional swimming	3
Gardening	11
The gym/PE	4
Cycling	2
Golf	2
Bowls	1
Building	1
Church cleaning	1
Church maintenance	1
Skiing	1
Table tennis	1

7.   LOOKING TO THE FUTURE

Have you made a will?

Yes:	47
No:	6

Have you given somebody a power of attorney (for health and/or for finance)?

Yes:	13
No:	40

Have you chosen hymns or readings for your funeral?

Yes:	20
Made suggestions	3
No:	30

Do you have any worries about the future?

Yes - worries	16
Yes - concerns	11
No:	26

8.   RELATIONSHIP WITH GOD

How regular are your daily devotions?

Every day	36
Most days	15
Infrequently	2

What scheme are you currently using for your personal reading of the Bible?

The Lectionary/Celtic Daily Prayer	8
Printed Bible reading notes	21
Online Bible notes/devotional thoughts	4
Reading through a Bible book with a commentary	13
Reading through a bible book without a commentary or notes	10
I don't have a regular pattern of reading	3

Are you accountable to anyone spiritually?

Yes:	13
No:	40

Is there anyone who serves as a mentor to you?

Yes:	11
No:	42

If no [to the two previous questions], would you see any benefit at this stage in having another person have input into your life?

Yes:	13
No:	24

Don't know:	2
No answer	14

Have you been able to continue some biblical and theological study?

Yes:	30
No:	23

Do you belong to a theological society or study group where you can grow and develop in your theological thinking?

Yes:	7
No:	46

9.   RELATIONSHIP WITH A LOCAL CHURCH

How happy are you in your present church?

Very happy:	18
Happy	10
OK	13
Unhappy	8
Very unhappy	2

How supportive is the church to you?

Very supportive	17
Supportive	14
I am treated like any other retired person	10
I feel I am ignored	6
I feel I am treated with suspicion	5
Yet to settle	1

How good is your relationship with the minister of your present church?

Very good	17
Good	13

OK	7
Not good	6
Not good at all	3
No minister	6
Yet to settle	1

How much do you feel part of your present church?

I feel very much part of the church	19
I feel quite part of the church	15
OK	6
I feel on the edge	7
I feel very much on the edge	3
Yet to settle	1

Do you belong to a home group or similar small group?

Yes:	34
No:	18
Yet to settle	1

Do you belong to other groups in the church?

Men's group/men's prayer breakfast	8
Deacon/elder/PCC	4
Prayer chain/prayer groups	3
Bible study group	2
The choir/the music group	2
Group for preaching	2
Group for planning worship	2
Group running Alpha	2
Group for exercising pastoral care	1
Group for publicity	1
Tea meeting for older people	2
Lunch club	1
Art & craft group	1

CAP job club	1
Messy church	1
Open Book (schools work)	1
Technical team	1
Maintenance team	1
None	21

10.   FRIENDS – IN THE CHURCH AND BEYOND THE CHURCH

Have you made friends with the members of the church?

Many:	19
[More than a few	4]
A few	25
None	4
Yet to settle	1

Have you made new friends outside the church?

Many:	12
A few	26
[Acquaintances	2]
None	5
No reply:	11

In the past six months how many church people have invited you into their home?

20+? (Most Sundays invited out for lunch)	1
Eight:	2
Six	2
Five	2
Four	3
Three or four	1
Two + invitation to a restaurant	1
Three	3

Two	9
One or two	1
Not many	2
One + invitation to a restaurant	1
One	5
None	17
No response	3

Are there any factors which make it difficult to make friends in the church?

Yes	18
No	35

11.   MINISTRY IN RETIREMENT

'God continues to have a call' versus 'the time to withdraw'

Ordination is for life, so God continues to have a call on my life:
43

Retirement is the time to withdraw from the demands of ministry
13

Content to be an ordinary 'punter' versus 'I find it difficult'

On Sundays I am content to be an ordinary 'punter' in the pew   22

I find it difficult listening to somebody else preach   22

Opportunities for the retired to serve God in his church

I continue to preach and lead Bible studies:	45
I look for opportunities to share my faith:	32
I continue to take funerals:	29
I lead a home/small group:	19
I help with pastoral care:	25
I mentor younger ministers:	10 + 1 "I used to"
I serve as a spiritual director:	1

12.   RELATIONSHIPS WITH OTHER MINISTERS SINCE RETIREMENT

Do you attend as local ministers meeting?

Yes: 5

No: 48

Do you belong to a retired ministers' group?

Yes: 33

No: 20

13.   RELATIONSHIPS WITH THE BU AND REGIONAL MINISTERS IN RETIREMENT

Have you had a pastoral visit or personal letter or phone call from your regional minister?

Yes: 11

No: 42

Respondents within the Eastern Baptist Association:

Yes: 5

No: 20

How often do you have opportunities to preach in churches in your Association?

None: 9

Once: 1

Rarely: 5

Occasionally   11

Once a month   4

Regularly   4

Twice a month   3

Very often   1

In one church   2

I do not seek them	5
My wife is ill	1
No longer	7

Have you served as a Moderator of another church?
Yes: 15
No: 38

Have you been asked to do any other task in another church?
Yes: 9
No: 44

Have you been to an association ministers' conference?
Yes: 13
No: 40

Have you been to the Baptist Assembly?
Yes: 14
No: 39

Have you been to an Association assembly?
Yes: 17
No: 36

Do you read the electronic Baptist Times?
Yes: 19
No: 34

How much do you feel part of the Baptist family?
I feel very much part of the wider Baptist family	2
I feel part of the wider Baptist family	21
I feel neither one thing nor another	15
I no longer feel part of the wider Baptist family	11

I feel forgotten by the wider Baptist family   8

Are you content with the support you currently receive?
Yes: 13
No: 40

14.   RELATIONSHIP WITH THE FAMILY

Involvement in church life
Number of children still involved in church life: 57
Number of children no longer involved in church life   60
Number of grandchildren attending church   114
Number of grandchildren not attending church   101

15.   RELATIONSHIP WITH THE WIDER WORLD

New Interests
I work as a volunteer in the community   21
I have developed new IT skills   10
I go [regularly] to the theatre, cinema, concert hall   9
I have done a cookery course   5
I have become a Rotarian (or equivalent)   4
I attend study courses linked with U3A/Workers Educational
Institute/ etc   4
I have joined a political party   3
I now belong to a book club: 2

16.   EXPERIENCE OF RETIREMENT SO FAR

What is the hardest challenge you face in retirement?
Growing older   8
Loneliness   6
Living life meaningfully   6
Time   5

Being a carer	4
Loss of role	4
Church	4
Money	1
No challenges	3

What are you still passionate about?

The Gospel	25
The Church	21
The Kingdom	19
Life	18
My family	6

General reflections on your experience of retirement

I am happy to be retired	39
Retirement has given me new opportunities to serve God	33
I am glad to pursue new interests outside the church	28
Retirement is an opportunity to relax and rest	24
Retirement has given opportunities to engage with the wider community	22
Retirement has given opportunities to make friends outside the church	22
Retirement has given opportunities to travel & see more of God's world	22
Retirement gives me opportunities for play	21
Retirement is a great adventure	20
In retirement I am busier than ever	10
Retirement has proved a lonely experience	8
Retirement has led to a restriction in life	7
In my retirement I am still searching for purpose	6
Retirement has proved fairly boring	4

The College of Baptist Ministers

The College of Baptist Ministers is a community of colleagues supporting and encouraging one another in Christian ministry in Baptist Churches in the UK.

CBM DEVELOPING MINISTRY

Resources and Training.

A regular newsletter.

Resources: academic and sabbatical studies, research, courses, documents and media.

Advisors sharing expertise and experience.

Sabbatical suggestions.

Peer mentoring and spiritual direction.

Guidelines & Facilitators for Reviews of Ministry.

Our nine-stranded approach to Continuing Ministerial Development with your own Personal CMD Portfolio.

Gifts and massive reductions on purchase prices of books on ministry.

CBM SUPPORT IN MINISTRY

Advice, Assistance and Support.

Code of Ethics in Ministry.

Guidelines and Policies on good practice.

Professional standing among colleagues and churches.

Telephone Helpline for Members.

CBM

college of baptist ministers

www.collegeofbaptistministers.com